ANGER MANAGEMENT

A Practical Resource for Children with Learning, Social and Emotional Difficulties

Fiona Burton and Melanie Wells

www.speechmark.net

ANGER MANAGEMENT

A Practical Resource for Children with Learning, Social and Emotional Difficulties

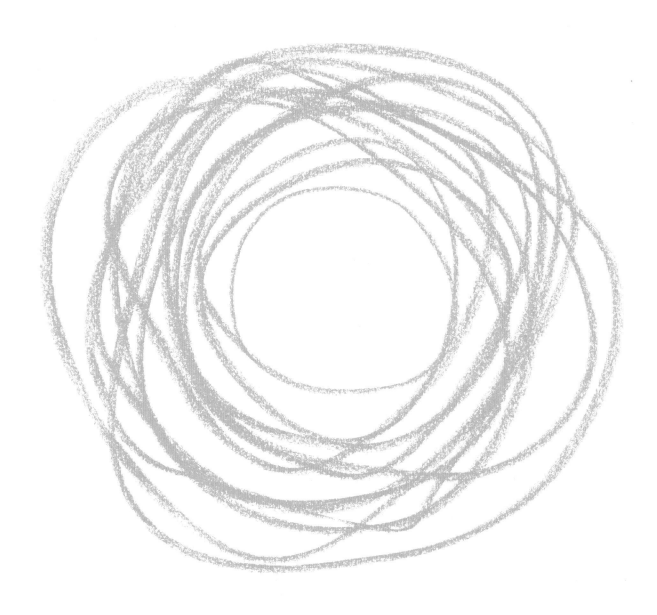

Published by

Speechmark Publishing Ltd, 70 Alston Drive, Bradwell Abbey, Milton Keynes MK13 9HG, UK
Tel: +44 (0)1908 326 944   Fax: +44 (0)1908 326 960

www.speechmark.net

002-5726 Printed in the United Kingdom by CMP (uk) Ltd.

British Library Cataloguing in Publication Data
A catalogue record for this book is available from the British Library

ISBN: 978 0 86388 811 3

Acknowledgements
Figures 3, 7 and 8 as referenced
Animal pictures – shark, hedgehog, bee, tortoise, dragon and spider copyright © Sarah Walbrin.
Cooperative puzzle – caveman beside the fire copyright © Emma Wells.
All other illustrations copyright © Melanie Wells and Fiona Burton.

Contents

Introduction

Aims of the resource

This resource aims to support pupils who have difficulties managing strong feelings and managing their behaviour. It develops self-belief about the ability to change and equips pupils with the skills to change.

The Every Child Matters Framework, Children Act 2004 and the launch of the Social and Emotional Aspects of Learning (SEAL) curriculum have highlighted the need for schools to nurture and cultivate children's social and emotional development. The Special Educational Needs Code of Practice provides practical advice to Local Authorities, education settings and others in supporting children's special educational needs.

Many children with language and/or learning difficulties also experience difficulties with social, emotional and behavioural development. Emotional literacy packages often contain worksheets, stories and abstract language concepts. Children who have difficulties with literacy, attention or speech and language may find it difficult to access many aspects of these packages. One of the aims of this resource is to deliver an appealing, practical and meaningful programme which all children (including those with learning difficulties) will find easy to access and enjoy. The concepts delivered in this resource have been simplified and aim to cater for different learning styles. Literacy elements have been reduced. Emphasis is given to practical approaches such as games and role plays. The resource is built around a visual model of anger (the firework model: Figure 1).

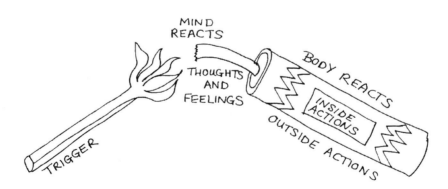

Figure 1   The firework model

The authors have used the resource in both mainstream and special schools (the latter for pupils with moderate learning difficulties or social, emotional or behavioural difficulties). The resource has been used with children to reduce the risk of exclusion and to support reintegration into mainstream schools.

This anger management resource is a complete set of materials to enable a facilitator to deliver an eight-week groupwork course. It has been designed to cover eight elements, which fit roughly within a half-term of weekly sessions. However, each session can be adapted and expanded over several weeks in order to provide more in-depth support.

The resource can be adapted for whole class groups or sessions with individual pupils but is designed to be used with small groups.

The pack contains ideas to help facilitators communicate the aims of the sessions to parents and pupils, including draft parental consent letters, information sheets about the programme, weekly parent feedback sheets about the sessions and practical ways to support the objectives for each session.

It also contains everything needed within the sessions, including plans for the facilitators, games and takeaway and follow-up activities. It includes debriefing notes for teachers to aid them in supporting follow-up activities and for helping children to generalise the new skills that they have been learning.

Links to Every Child Matters outcomes

This resource supports each of the 5 'Every Child Matters' outcomes, which aims for all children whatever their background or circumstances, to:

- *Be healthy*
  The sessions promote emotional well-being through recognising and developing understanding of different feelings and learning how to manage these.

- *Stay safe*
  The sessions help pupils to manage strong feelings safely, encourage them to listen to and consider the views of others, and develop pro-social behaviour.

- *Enjoy and achieve*
  Academic achievement and social and emotional development have been shown to be strongly linked. The sessions aim to enhance pupils' social, emotional and behavioural development so that they experience success and are more able to access learning opportunities.

- *Make a positive contribution*
  Negative behaviours and pro-social alternatives are explored throughout this course. Developing skills of anger management supports the development of positive relationships. The programme also aims to develop pupils' self-esteem and confidence by helping them to identify their strengths and skills.

- *Achieve economic well-being*
  The resource has been used to reduce the risk of exclusion and support reintegration into school. It aims to develop behavioural and social skills that can be used throughout life.

Links to SEAL

This resource covers many objectives within the SEAL curriculum and can be used to provide additional intensive support in these areas.

The resource complements the 'new beginnings' and 'going for goals' SEAL themes. Pupils are asked what they would like to gain from the programme. They are encouraged to track their changes (eg through diaries, blogs, graphs and pre- and post-intervention measures).

The SEAL theme of 'relationships' is developed by encouraging pupils to reflect on different feelings (eg feelings bingo, feelings blogs). Sessions encourage pupils to take responsibility for their actions and understand how others might be hurt by them (by, for example, exploring different scenarios through role plays or the use of puppets).

The resource particularly builds on the 'getting on and falling out' SEAL theme. The concept of looking at things from another perspective is demonstrated through the use of visual illusions and role plays. The firework model (Figure 1) is used to illustrate triggers for anger, the link between thoughts, feelings and actions, and physiological responses to anger. Animal analogies are used to explore short- and long-term consequences of behaviour. Pupils are encouraged to talk about different strategies for managing strong feelings.

The resource complements the 'good to be me' SEAL theme (particularly in the self-esteem session) by encouraging pupils to reflect on their personal strengths and practise giving each other compliments.

CHAPTER 1
What is anger management?

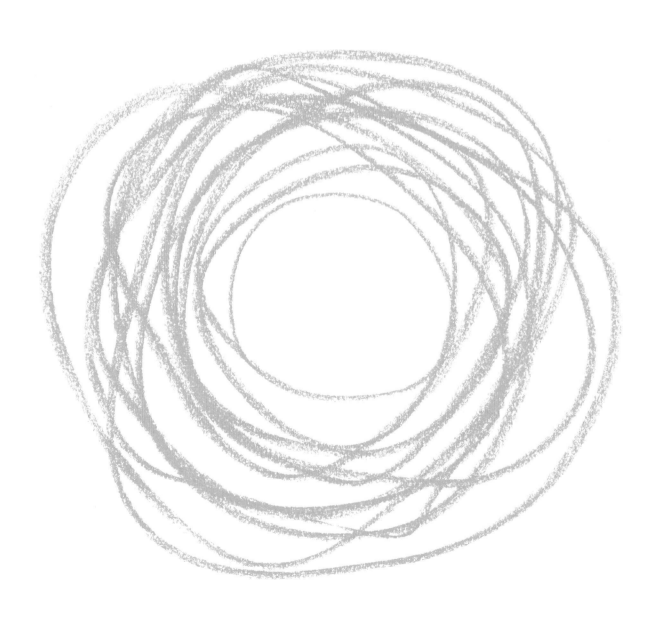

CHAPTER 1

What is anger management?

Why do we feel?

This resource is all about feelings. Feelings are what make us human. Emotions are something we all share and can identify with. Emotions can influence what we do. They can spur us into action or stop us in our tracks. Feeling angry can sometimes cause us to withdraw from a situation in frustration, or it can lead us to fight for others and against injustice. Feeling sad can cause us to give up hope and stop trying, or it can move us to help others. Goleman (1998) claimed that the ability to read and understand our emotions is a crucial life skill. He maintained that emotional intelligence is more important than any other form of intelligence. It has a greater impact on all kinds of personal, career and school successes.

Goleman found that emotional intelligence could be divided into two main skills: personal competence (how we handle ourselves) and social competence (how we handle relationships). Personal competence includes self-awareness (our understanding of ourselves), motivation (our ability to set and achieve goals) and self-regulation (being able to manage our feelings). Social competence involves empathy (understanding how others may be feeling) and social skills (adapting our behaviour to take the needs of others into account). You might recognise these five skills from the SEAL curriculum.

This resource focuses on self-regulation, that is, our ability to manage our feelings and not allow them to overwhelm or control us.

Why do we feel angry?

Dictionary definitions of anger tend to describe annoyance and/or displeasure. However, anger is an emotion that varies in intensity from mild annoyance to rage or fury.

Anger tends to be a secondary emotion which is triggered by other feelings (eg frustration, fear, embarrassment, sorrow). We generally feel angry when we are threatened. Threats can take many different forms. We can be threatened physically or emotionally. Our pride can feel threatened when someone disagrees with us. Our sense of safety can be threatened when someone is unkind to us. Our sense of justice is threatened when we are treated unfairly. Feeling threatened can cause us to feel angry.

Anger is a particularly strong emotion. When we feel angry our body reacts in lots of ways. It recognises that we are under threat and therefore prepares us for action (Figure 2). Typically we react by either defending ourselves and fighting the threat (fight) or retreating from the threat to safety (flight). In either case we need to respond quickly. Delayed responses could result in being harmed by the threat.

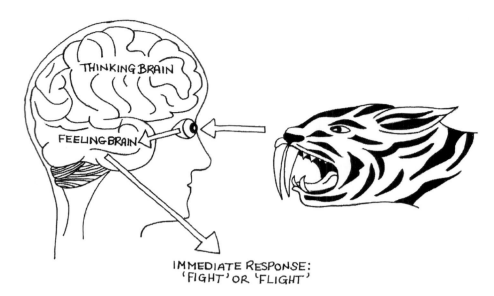

Figure 2   Fight or flight response

When we feel threatened our sympathetic nervous system is activated. This leads to a release of stress hormones (eg adrenaline, noraderenaline and cortisol) into the bloodstream. These chemicals cause a range of reactions in the body, including:

- dilation of the airways and rapid breathing (in order to increase oxygenation of the blood)
- increased sweating (eg clammy palms)
- heart beating harder and faster
- muscles tensing, ready for action
- goosepimples
- reduced capacity for rational thought and language (it is believed) as the brain focuses on preparing for action.

These reactions happen automatically when stress hormones are released. In the short-term these reactions are helpful as they prepare the body for action. However, if the system is overused (eg when a person endures long-lasting periods of threat) the reaction can become harmful. For example, it can lead to:

- difficulty in relaxing and therefore sleeping
- an inability to concentrate on other things
- feeling emotionally overwhelmed
- hypervigilance (constantly on the look out for danger)
- palpitations
- increased blood pressure
- prolonged muscle tension leading to headaches, muscular or skeletal problems and exhaustion
- increased cortisol output leading to a depressed immune system, resulting in vulnerability to illness.

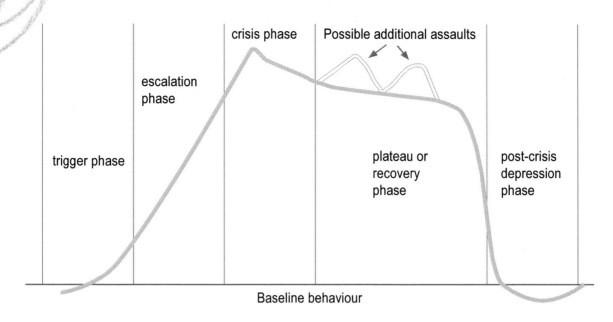

Figure 3   The assault cycle (*Source*: Breakwell, 1997)

Figure 3 is a representation of what happens when we feel angry. The baseline reflects our normal level of arousal. When something happens that triggers angry feelings our arousal increases quickly. Unless anger is controlled at an early stage it reaches a crisis point (triggering fight or flight). It is easiest to intervene at the earliest stage. Attention can be averted. The pupil may need to be relocated. They may need to be given some time and space to take up directions. They may need to access calming activities or be encouraged to use calming strategies (eg relaxation techniques, physical activity, time out). At crisis stage the focus will be on making the situation safe. It is important that any intervention is non-threatening. Directions should be delivered calmly using simple language. Recovery can be very slow. Even when a pupil looks calm their adrenaline and arousal levels can still be very high. This means that it is easy for a very small trigger to cause further crises. It can take a few hours for an arousal level to return to baseline levels. Discussion of the incident should be avoided during the recovery phase as this could easily increase the pupil's already high levels of arousal. If an outburst has been very severe a pupil may enter a post-crisis depression phase where they feel very low and upset and regret their actions. At this time they will need reassurance and to be given the message that they are accepted despite their unacceptable behaviour.

Is anger OK?

Anger is a natural human emotion. It has a purpose. Anger can be motivating and help to spur us into action. History is teeming with people whose anger led to good. William Wilberforce's anger led to the abolition of slavery. Martin Luther King's anger led to the end of racial segregation. Without anger would they have found the strength to persist against immense difficulties? Anger can trigger a fight for justice. Anger can lead us to help others. Anger can motivate us to stand up to a bully. Anger can lead us to do what is right.

Anger can also cause us to do what we later regret (particularly as it often leads us to act impulsively). Sometimes we harm others in our fight to protect ourselves. Anger can lead to harsh words. Anger can lead to retribution and violence.

So, anger can result in good or it can lead to harm. Anger is a natural human emotion. Without it we may lack the motivation to act and the strength to persist. How we choose to manage anger is the crucial factor.

> Anyone can become angry – that is easy. But to be angry with the right person, to the right degree, at the right time, for the right purpose, and in the right way – this is not easy.
>
> (Aristotle, quoted in Goleman, 1995 p ix)

How are thoughts, feelings and behaviour linked?

The way we think about a situation can change the way we feel about it, and the way we feel about a situation can change the way that we respond to it.

Imagine you have a very busy day ahead. You have been up half the night preparing resources and plans for work the next day. When you arrive at work you find that your colleague has not prepared some of the resources that you need, as was agreed. How do you feel? Angry? Why? Probably because you are thinking it is unfair that they have not done their share of the work. You might be thinking that they are lazy or that they don't care about your workload. How might you react? You might complain or refuse to do your share of the work next time. Now imagine that you find out that they had been up all night with their sick child. How do you feel? Why might you feel less angry? The situation has not changed … the work has still not been done. Things are just as difficult for you. However, your thoughts about the situation are likely to be very different. You might be thinking that it is not their fault because they could not both look after their chid and complete the work. Those kinds of thoughts change the feelings you are likely to have. You might feel sorry for your colleague. Those feelings influence your behaviour. You are now much less likely to complain and more likely to ask if there is anything you can do to help them.

Thoughts, feelings and behaviour are inextricably linked. They are linked together like the carriages of a train (Figure 4). The thoughts drive the feelings and the behaviour follows on behind.

Figure 4   Thoughts–feelings–behaviour

Behaviour is always based on preceding feelings and thoughts. When a child reacts aggressively there will always be an influencing feeling and thought. Cognitive behavioural psychology has found that if we can identify the thoughts and feelings behind behaviour we can work with them to bring about change that will result in different behaviour. Understanding the thoughts and feelings underlying a behaviour will also help us understand how to respond.

Why might children find it difficult to manage anger?

We are not born with the ability to manage our feelings. When a baby is hungry it cries. It does not immediately think 'I don't need to panic or cry because milk is on its way'. Yet over time this is exactly what the baby learns. Babies develop an ability to manage their uncomfortable feelings through their trust in adults who consistently meet their needs. As a toddler grows older they become more and more sophisticated in their understanding of relationships and feelings. They learn to wait. They learn to solve problems. Sometimes, however, parents find it very difficult to recognise and consistently provide for their child's needs. Over time this makes it difficult for the child to trust that their needs will be met. They therefore have trouble managing difficult feelings because they often have not experienced that things will work out all right.

Children learn by watching, interacting with and copying others. Sometimes children's role models have difficulty managing their own feelings. They might explode with aggression or they might bottle up their feelings. Watching role models repeatedly handle situations in a particular way can lead children to learn to deal with situations in a similar manner.

Figure 5   Children learn by watching and copying others

As we have seen, behaviour has a purpose. Behaviour is about getting a need met. It is an attempt to solve a problem. Maslow (1943) developed a hierarchy of needs which outlines the sorts of needs we try to meet (Figure 6).

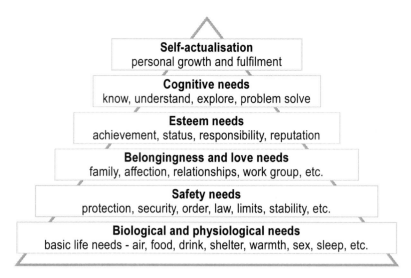

Figure 6   Maslow's hierarchy of human needs

Our most basic needs are at the bottom of the pyramid (biological and physiological needs such as those for food, drink and sleep). The needs become more and more sophisticated as they progress up the pyramid. Maslow suggested that we will have a high level of motivation to get our most basic of needs met before we experience high levels of motivation to get more sophisticated needs met. Interestingly, cognitive needs are at the top of the pyramid. This indicates that much of what schools promote, for example, the need to learn and achieve, are underpinned by more fundamental needs such as feeling safe, belonging and esteem. Sometimes children may behave in challenging ways because they are trying to get a need met (and possibly don't know how else to do this).

Some children have been through many difficult experiences and have a lot to rightly feel angry about. Some children, for example, have experienced multiple bereavements, parental separation, neglect, abuse, the imprisonment of a parent, eviction or domestic violence. If a child lives permanently in a state of high arousal their feelings of anger and anxiety can be overwhelming and difficult for them to deal with.

The aim of this programme is to enable children to:

* develop skills to recognise and reflect on their feelings
* recognise that feeling angry is not wrong – it is often right (but can sometimes be handled better)
* understand that thoughts can power up anger or can defuse it
* learn alternative ways of managing strong feelings.

If children can learn to manage difficult feelings they are likely to experience better relationships. They are likely to feel less stressed and anxious and are more likely to attend school. Their behaviour may become less challenging, leading to fewer exclusions. Children are likely to be readier to learn and therefore likely to achieve more. These benefits are likely to impact on school ethos, pupil and staff morale and community well-being.

References

Breakwell G (1997) Coping with Aggressive Behaviour, British Psychological Society, Leicester.

Goleman D (1995) *Emotional Intelligence: Why It Can Matter More Than IQ*, Bloomsbury, London.

Goleman D (1998) *Working with Emotional Intelligence*, Bloomsbury, London.

Maslow AH (1943) 'A theory of human motivation', *Psychological Review*, 50 (4), pp370–96.

CHAPTER 2
How can we help children to develop anger management skills?

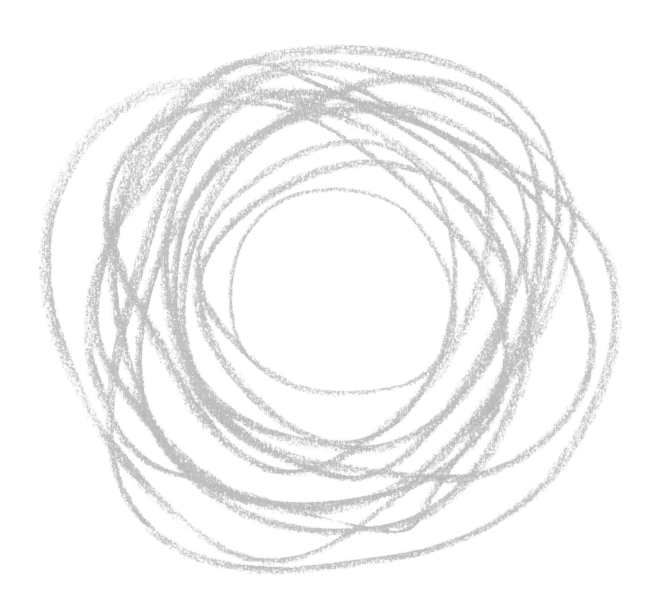

CHAPTER 2

How can we help children to develop anger management skills?

Stages of change

Developing anger management skills involves change. Change is rarely easy and is often a long process. A pupil needs to decide that they want to change before they can put that commitment into action. A pupil cannot be made to change against their will. Attempting to do so can be counter-productive and can lead to pupils ignoring our efforts or feeling angry at not being listened to. Therefore providing an anger management intervention is likely to be far more effective in producing change if pupils have already recognised the need for change and are committed to the process.

To help children change and to move forward we need to establish exactly where they are in the change process. Prochaska & DiClemente (1982) created a model that describes the stages we go through as we change. The model can be used to establish where a pupil is within a change process in order to inform the support they need to move forward. This is illustrated in Figure 7.

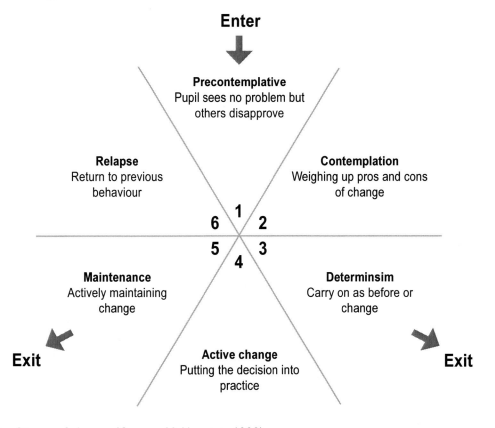

Figure 7   Stages of change (*Source*: McNamara, 1998)

In stage 1 the pupil does not demonstrate awareness of the problem that others recognise. For example, they may not be aware that their behaviour is causing a problem for themselves or others. Alternatively, they may have given up on the possibility of change because the problem has been going on for so long that it feels normal. In this stage the focus of support is reflecting on whether behaviour is a problem. It is important to give pupils a lot of time to do this – through talking about the specifics of the behaviour (when, where, how), talking about consequences, promoting positive feelings of self, exploring barriers to change and talking about exceptions (when the behaviour is or is not a problem). At this stage the pupil should not be encouraged to make a decision about whether or not to change. If they are not given sufficient opportunity to think about change they will not make an informed decision at the appropriate stage and may carry unresolved difficulties.

In stage 2 the pupil is aware of the problem. However, they have not decided whether they should change. Working through stage 2 involves weighing up the pros and cons of changing. For example, a pupil may feel that if they were to change their behaviour there might be benefits such as keeping their parents happy, doing better in school and receiving fewer detentions. They may also recognise some costs of changing, such as needing to work hard, losing their reputation with peers and no longer being perceived as powerful. It is important that the pupil is given enough time to explore this phase fully. Moving too fast may lead to barriers to change not being explored and therefore becoming a problem later on. For example, pupils may agree to change their behaviour and then present again with the same old behaviour within days.

In stage 3 the pupil decides whether or not to change. If they decide to change they will need to develop an action plan to support the change. This should contain short targets that they can measure their progress against. It should contain strategies that will be used when things get difficult. If the pupil decides that the costs of change are too great they exit the process. If the pupil has been given time to explore all the issues, adults can be more confident that the pupil has made an informed decision. If at a later point the pupil decides they would like to re-evaluate the possibility of change, they would re-enter the model at stage 2. During the planning phase of stage 3 pupils decide what they will do, and identify any potential obstacles and what would be appropriate responses to them.

The anger management intervention is likely to be most effective when pupils have committed to change (stages 3–4). The aim of the intervention is to increase pupils' knowledge about the behaviour they have decided to change and equip them with the skills to maintain the change.

During stage 4 the pupil starts putting their action plan into practice. Pupils in stage 4 often need a lot of support to implement their plan and not give up at the first hurdle. They may need regular meetings to review their progress, celebrate successes, solve difficulties and boost motivation.

During stage 5 support can gradually be reduced as the pupil is able to maintain change more independently. However, they may still need opportunities to 'check in' and to review how things have been going. As the pupil maintains change, support can be withdrawn. The model is very realistic in that it acknowledges that people may relapse and return to previous behaviour (stage 6). If this occurs they can work through the change process again. It is also possible for a pupil to move backwards from a stage. This might indicate a need for more work at a previous stage.

What does this model mean for anger management programmes in school? If we tell children they need to complete an anger management programme without asking for their thoughts about that and without establishing where they are in the process of change, we are less likely to see long-lasting change. We need to establish first whether the pupil is aware that their behaviour may be causing a problem, whether they recognise change may come with a cost and whether they feel that the potential benefits of change outweigh the costs. If we rush through this process we risk leaving the pupil behind. Participating in an anger management programme will be less likely to produce change if the pupil has not decided themselves that they are ready for it. We have found that pupils who are not ready for change need instead to work through the possibility of changing before starting an anger management programme.

The decision to change does not produce change in itself. A lack of skills and knowledge may be a barrier to change. Therefore to change we also need to develop new skills and learn to do things differently. Learning is often a long process.

Learning new skills

Haring & Eaton (1978) developed a hierarchy that demonstrates the process we go through when we learn a new skill (Figure 8).

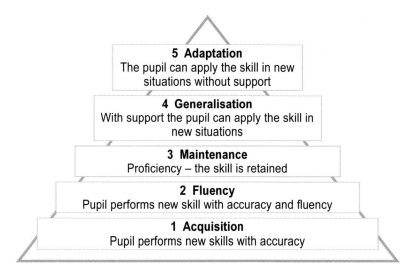

Figure 8   Learning hierarchy (*Source*: Haring & Eaton, 1978)

When we learn a new skill we initially focus on developing our understanding of the skill and using it accurately (getting it right). In the anger management programme one of the skills covered is looking at a situation from another perspective. Initially pupils are taught that there are often multiple perspectives to a situation. They practise identifying perspectives in different situations. As the skill develops they move on to the second stage of learning. This involves becoming more fluent. During this stage the pupil becomes more confident and quicker at identifying different perspectives. The next stage is to then apply the skill in new situations, with support (eg to apply the skill in a real classroom situation). Finally, when the skill is fully secure the pupil is able to automatically apply the skill in new situations without any support.

What does this model mean for an anger management programme? When a pupil is developing a new skill they need lots of opportunities to practise it. Psychologists often call this 'over-learning'. The more we practise, the more secure the skill becomes and the less likely we are to forget it. If we were to practise the skill only once a week and not use it in between, we would be much more likely to forget the skill. This programme therefore includes a follow-up activity between every session. The purpose of this activity is to encourage pupils to practise the skill they have been learning during the week (in order to help the skill become secure). The programme also includes teacher debriefing notes. The aim of the notes is to outline the skills being taught that week and to give teachers some ideas about how they could encourage further development of the skill (reinforcement) and provide opportunities for practice.

With practice a skill can be learned so well that it is never forgotten (a little like riding a bike). New behaviours become the norm. What does this tell us about how children learn to manage their feelings? The model shows that learning a new skill is a long process that involves several stages. Sometimes staff expect children to change radically on completion of the programme. While this does sometimes happen, it is not the norm. We have used the model to show staff that teaching skills through the anger management programme is only the first step in learning to change. Pupils will need lots of practice and reinforcement. This helps to create realistic expectations of pupils. It also encourages staff to think about ways they can build on the programme in class.

Social learning (role models)

Social psychology has found that children learn through watching others. They learn by copying role models. Many children have experienced and are reproducing very negative cycles of behaviour. School provides opportunities to explore alternative positive behaviours. This happens most effectively through modelling behaviour rather than teaching it. To learn new behaviours they need to be modelled consistently. Therefore children need to not just be taught skills of anger management but to observe these skills in others.

Positive reinforcement

Behavioural psychology has found that behaviour can be changed through reinforcement. If we reinforce the behaviour we want to increase through praise, attention and rewards, children are likely to display more of it in order to experience more of the positive reinforcements. Therefore if we reinforce a child each time they demonstrate a skill in anger management, they will be more likely to use the skill again.

Why is a whole school approach needed?

Children learn best when they are surrounded by the same message. Different, conflicting messages are confusing. Therefore anger management programmes are likely to be most effective when they are embedded in the school ethos. This means everyone that a pupil comes into contact with needs to recognise that anger results from feeling threatened and that any behaviour is preceded by needs, thoughts and feelings. So all staff need to model appropriate ways to handle difficult feelings. They should all use language that the child is familiar with (eg thoughts, feelings, triggers, fuses). The more these messages become the norm the more likely the child is to understand and learn them.

A whole school approach to anger management and emotional literacy are likely to be more effective in producing change. This means reflecting values not just in group sessions but also throughout the curriculum, in behaviour policies, in pastoral support plans, in attitudes and conversations.

A whole school approach means reflecting on school-wide questions such as:

* Do all staff model the skills they want children to learn?

* Is the culture one in which it is safe to try something new and take risks without fear of judgement?

* Is everyone helped to feel included and that they belong? Is everyone listened to?

* Are pupils and staff given opportunities and space to calm down when they feel angry?

* Are pupils and staff encouraged to understand the thoughts and feelings of others?

* Are people given positive feedback and opportunities to reflect on and develop their strengths?

* Does the behaviour policy and the approach to discipline encourage pupils and staff to reflect on their feelings and manage them appropriately?

* Do staff make it clear that it is the inappropriate behaviour that is unwanted, not the pupil themselves?

* Are expectations of everyone realistic, clear and positive?

Looking after ourselves

Working with difficult behaviour can be very challenging. It can use all our mental energy, leaving us feeling frustrated and even angry. It is therefore important for us to take care of ourselves in order to be able to take care of others.

Some ways in which we can look after ourselves are:

* Working with a colleague will enable us to receive feedback about how things are going and bounce ideas off each other.

* Talking with others about behaviour can help us to gain new insight into what may be behind particular behaviours.

* Recognising when things feel too tough and allowing another to take over can help us to step back to reflect when needed.

* Talking with others about difficult situations can help us to solve problems and find a new way forward.

* Taking time out and achieving a good work–life balance can help us to unwind and rejuvenate. It is important for us to take care of ourselves in order to be able to take care of others.

Supporting each other will help us to be in a better place to support the pupils we work with.

References

McNamara E (1998) 'Motivational interviewing: the theory and practice of eliciting pupil motivation', Positive Behaviour Management.

Haring NG & Eaton MD (1978) 'Systematic procedures: an instructional hierarchy', Haring NG, Lovitt TC, Eaton MD, Hansen CL (eds.), The Fourth R: Research in the Classroom, Merrill Columbus, OH.

CHAPTER 3
Introduction to the eight-session model

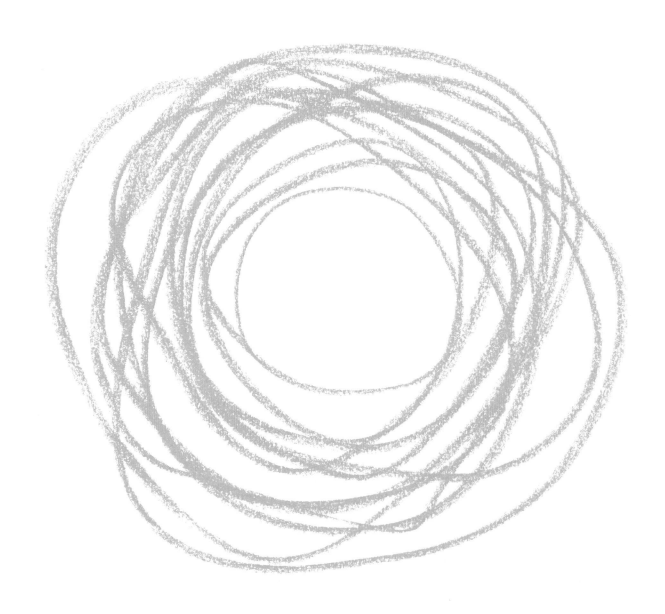

CHAPTER 3
Introduction to the eight-session model

Previous chapters have outlined the reasons why some pupils might find it difficult to manage anger or self-regulate their emotions. Understanding the complex issues that have impacted on the pupil's ability to learn these skills makes it clear why working with these pupils on anger management strategies alone will not be successful. It is the equivalent of putting a roof on a house that has no walls or foundations. The eight-week model, however, contains core elements that build a structure of knowledge and self-efficacy that helps the young person to develop the skills necessary to be able to manage their anger more successfully.

The model acknowledges that pupils will have insecure attachments and unmet needs and in some cases will be living in an environment where they have good reason to be angry. They may have learning difficulties that mean that they find anger management and self-regulation skills particularly difficult. Therefore the anger management course is not something that is done to pupils to remedy a deficit that they are responsible for but is delivered in the spirit of trying to support some of your most needy and vulnerable pupils.

Each of the following core elements around which each session is based is a vital and necessary ingredient in supporting the pupil.

1   Understanding anger
2   Understanding feelings
3   Self-esteem
4   Triggers and fuses
5   Learning to think differently
6   Physiology and relaxation
7   Strategies to manage anger
8   Review and reinforce

In the next section we will look at why each of these core elements is so important.

Session 1   Understanding anger

This session teaches the pupils the fight/flight model of anger. This helps them to understand that anger is a normal emotion and has a function. Some pupils may have been in situations where their lack of control during an angry outburst was extremely frightening. They may have felt that they could have seriously hurt or even killed someone, and this can reinforce the feeling that they are a bad person and increase their lack of self-esteem. Just hearing the caveman story can help the pupil to make sense of some of their most powerful feelings. Discussion about when these responses can be helpful (and indeed about historical cases where injustice elicited anger, such as apartheid and the disempowerment of women) can help to normalise anger and show that it is not the emotion itself that is destructive but how we sometimes behave in response to it.

Session 2   Understanding feelings

This session helps the pupils to increase their emotional literacy, as anger is often what we call a 'secondary emotion', that is, there is often a feeling that comes before it. If the pupil can successfully identify, name and verbalise these feelings, it will help them to recognise and manage the anger that accompanies it. The session helps pupils to identify good feelings and uncomfortable feelings. There can be some discussion around feeling 'tired' and whether this is a good feeling or an uncomfortable one: if you're in class trying to concentrate on a lesson, it is an uncomfortable feeling; however, if you're in bed trying to sleep, it can be a good feeling. This topic can lead to a discussion around sleep hygiene and the impact of lack of sleep on a pupil's ability to manage anger. Many pupils we work with do not have healthy or adequate sleep routines and this may impact on their ability to self-regulate. The pupils learn to label and define feelings by playing the feelings bingo game. This game will help the course facilitator to identify those pupils who have poor emotional literacy skills. The students may struggle to distinguish between feelings such as 'shock' and 'surprise' or with the meaning of 'lonely' as opposed to 'being alone'.

Session 3   Self-esteem

This session helps the pupils to think about their strengths and skills. For some it may be a new and even challenging experience to reflect on their positive qualities, and they may need considerable help from the group facilitator, using the materials suggested. However, this work is vital because until a pupil can recognise their skills and resources, they are unlikely to believe that change is possible and that they will be able to achieve the course aim of managing their anger more appropriately. This session will also build their resilience and resourcefulness. It will help them to separate their negative behaviour from their internal qualities and characteristics so that they can believe in themselves and their capacity for change.

Session 4   Triggers and fuses

This session builds on the pupils' emotional literacy vocabulary, with them listing anger words and ordering them by intensity. This will help pupils to increase their self-awareness and give them a structure to recognise when anger builds up. They are reintroduced to the firework model to help them understand the process of anger and how it affects them. Pupils start to think of situations that trigger their anger. These triggers may actually be linking to personal qualities discussed in the last session (eg loyalty to friends and family if criticising a friend or family member triggers anger). This can then also be linked back to the caveman story. Pupils can reflect on the way the fight/flight response is triggered when we perceive a threat to family or friends. The elements of this session build on the work of previous sessions, helping the pupils to integrate and assimilate skills. It also introduces them to the idea that it is not the situation or trigger that is responsible for their anger, but how they perceive and react to the trigger.

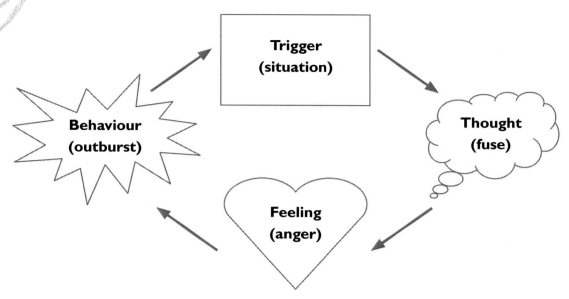

Figure 9   The thought–feeling–behaviour cycle

Session 5   Learning to think differently

This session builds on the previous ones by focusing on the fuse part of the firework model (see Figure 9). The optical illusions are a fun way of introducing the concept that there are two ways of viewing a situation. The session is based on a CBT (cognitive behaviour therapy) model.

It shows that by changing the thought and the feeling, the behaviour can change. It is often very difficult for pupils to access the thought part of the process and they will often name the feeling or jump straight to naming the behaviour. For example:

Facilitator: 'What would you be thinking if someone called you a name?'

Pupil: 'I would think I'm going to hit them.'

It may be necessary to spend some time on additional activities to help the pupils to access these negative automatic cognitions that lead to angry feelings and behaviour.

Once they have grasped the concept of this session you can discuss with the pupils how much more powerful they will be if they carefully choose the way they react to a person who is provoking them, rather than allowing that person to 'pull their strings'. You will be empowering the pupils to have control over their feelings and behaviour.

This is important because if people are experiencing intense feelings of anger but are not expressing them, they are likely to be bottling up feelings which may later explode.

Session 6   Physiology and relaxation

This session consolidates some of the work in the previous session and looks at the physiological responses that accompany angry feelings. It helps the pupils to recognise when they are getting angry. It also gives the pupils some strategies to manage angry feelings (eg breathing and relaxation techniques). These help the pupils to increase their awareness of their own body's physical responses to stressors and how they can manage these.

Session 7   Strategies to manage anger

In this penultimate session the pupils are helped to develop their own plans for managing their angry feelings and replacing those previous responses where they may hurt themselves, others or property.

By this point in the programme the pupils should have built up the skills, knowledge and resources to be able to put these strategies in place. They will also think about which strategies they can use in which context.

Session 8   Review and reinforce

In this session the pupils review whether their plans have been successful or whether they need rethinking or adjusting. The session also builds on all the work on self-awareness by helping the pupils consider how their behaviour impacts on others and how in turn that will impact on how others behave towards them.

It also teaches them a basic social communication skill: how to apologise to others. This is something they may have found very difficult, if not impossible, to do in the past. You can also help pupils to learn how to apologise in situations where they believe they are in the right but express their anger and frustration in an inappropriate way.

CHAPTER 4
Facilitating groupwork

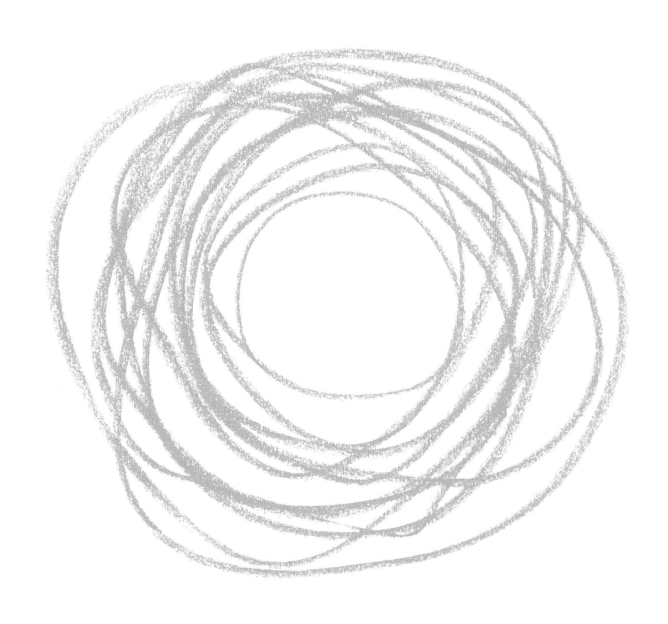

CHAPTER 4
Facilitating groupwork

The advantages of groupwork

Pupils benefit in several ways from being members of a supportive group led by a skilled facilitator as opposed to working individually. The small group setting gives them a safe environment to explore self-regulation issues, develop self-esteem and practise new skills. Being in a group gives more opportunity during the learning process to develop ways of relating to others. Pupils, particularly adolescents, are known to be particularly tuned in to the views and opinions of their peer group, so a positive group can enhance the learning experience.

However, there may be some pupils who are not able to manage the groupwork experience straight away and these materials can be used to support individual pupils as well as groups.

Sometimes it can be helpful to work with two pupils who can't cope with a group individually at first and then work with them as a pair, to help them to build up to working with a small group.

How many pupils should be in the group?

Having the right number of pupils in the group is important. We suggest six pupils maximum. When working with pupils with special needs who have difficulties with self-regulation, it is not a good idea to have so many in the group that it becomes a behaviour management exercise and the group facilitators are so taken up with crowd control that little teaching or learning can take place. You want this to be a group where pupils can take on board skills that can help them to change, so you want your energy to go into teaching these skills.

Who should facilitate the group?

We suggest two facilitators to four to six pupils. Having two group facilitators gives staff the opportunity to model appropriate interaction and behaviour towards each other to the pupils and help to set the norms for behaviour in the group. It also means that facilitators have peer support with the difficult task of groupwork, someone with whom to reflect and problem solve any issues that arise in the group.

The facilitators should prioritise the running of the group. The group should not be expendable because of other demands, as this will undermine the principles of valuing the pupils enough to support them in learning vital self-regulation skills. If the group is sacrificed for staff to cover other duties, it will give the message that the group, and therefore the pupils themselves, are unimportant.

The role of the group facilitator

The group facilitator needs to:

- have taken the time to have familiarised themselves with the programme materials
- be able to model good social, emotional and behavioural skills
- be skilled at being able to form trusting, positive relationships with the pupils in the group, even when the pupils' behaviour is challenging
- have some experience of working with groups and knowledge of group processes
- be reliable, consistent and able to provide a safe and positive environment for the members of the group
- be able to provide clear boundaries for the group
- have a basic knowledge of safeguarding children and be clear what action to take should child protection issues arise
- be reflective and able to adapt and respond to the needs of the group.

Which pupils will benefit from the group?

These may be pupils suggested by teaching staff and they may come from different classes. There are several questions that you need to ask about pupils who are put forward for the group:

- Are they good attendees?
- Are they well motivated?
- Do all of them get on together?
- Are they of a similar cognitive ability?

If the answer to any of these questions is 'no', you need to think how this will be managed.

Because the core elements of the programme that make up each of the sessions are all essential building blocks in learning how to manage anger appropriately, pupils will be at a disadvantage if they miss any of the sessions. Ideally, the pupil may be able to receive individual input to 'catch up' the session they missed; otherwise it can be useful to ask the other pupils to recap the learning themes from the previous session, thus reinforcing their understanding of the session as well as introducing it to the pupil who has missed it. But ideally pupils put forward for the group should be ones known to attend school regularly.

Once the prospective attendees of the group have been identified, it is essential that they are prepared for the group. Do they recognise that managing their anger is a problem for them as well as for others? Are they motivated to do something about it? Are they committed to attending the group and doing the daily activities that support the weekly sessions?

It is helpful to meet each pupil individually to assess their difficulties and their readiness for the group. It is also important to be aware of some of their personal circumstances. For example, do they long to spend more time with an absent father? Have they spent time in care? Are they frustrated, coping with a learning difficulty such as dyslexia? Are they caring for a parent with alcoholism? When running a group with pupils who may be vulnerable, this kind of information can raise awareness of sensitive issues that could arise in a group where pupils are discussing feelings and anger.

Running the group

Pre- and post-group assessments and measuring outcomes

There are several ways that you can measure the impact of the groupwork.

We include in this resource copies of a pre-intervention interview sheet and also a pupil's evaluation of intervention sheet. These can be used to obtain the pupils' qualitative and quantitative assessment of the value and impact of the groupwork.

We also include a self-regulation matrix that can be used to score the pupil's progress against the session's learning objectives.

How often should the group meet?

The course involves weekly input of about 45 minutes. It includes follow-on work to do in between sessions, so there will need to be someone who can support the pupil daily for a few minutes to complete this. This does not need to be one of the group facilitators.

Where should the group meet?

It is very important to have a designated place or room to meet weekly. It is helpful if this is a special place where you just meet for the group and it should be booked so that it is available every week. It should also be somewhere where you are unlikely to be disturbed during the group session (eg the photocopier room is a bad idea), and it is a good idea to have a 'Do Not Disturb' sign on the door during the group sessions. This will help the group to feel safe and valued.

How can other school staff support the group?

Groupwork will not be successful unless it is fully supported by the pupils' respective class teachers. The class teacher should have an understanding of the aims of the programme. The teacher's feedback sheets inform the class teacher of the support that is needed to reinforce the session. It is the teacher's responsibility to make sure that the follow-on activities are completed. If possible they should find whole class opportunities to reinforce the learning objectives of the groupwork session. There are many aspects of the programme that may have learning opportunities for all children in the class, and if there are any chances for the group member to share these with the class in a positive way it can be a way of building their resilience and self-efficacy as well as increasing the skills of the other class members.

The head teacher and senior leadership team can support the group by ensuring that staff time for the group is prioritised and protected and that the work is high profile and valued by all staff in the school. It is important that the groupwork is seen as an integral part of the school curriculum to support the pupils' learning, not an 'add on' or a luxury to be sacrificed when human resources are stretched.

How can difficult behaviour in the group be managed?

If you have a group of pupils who all have self-regulation difficulties, it stands to reason that these are also pupils who will have difficulties managing their behaviour and may need support in doing this during the sessions.

Group rules

The first activity in the group is deciding the group rules. Discussing them with the members of the group gives them ownership of the agreed rules, emphasising that they are something they have all signed up to, not something imposed on them. However, the group should be encouraged to keep the group rules simple and limited to about three.

They could include:

- Listen to each other.
- Be kind to each other.
- Keep what is said in the group in the group.

Or:

- Only one person talks at a time.
- Respect each other.
- Have fun without stopping others from learning.

Introduce the fact that rewards or tokens can be earned by pupils keeping these simple group rules.

Structure of the sessions

The structure of the sessions is always consistent so the pupils know what to expect. Each session starts with a reminder of the group rules and how tokens, and in turn, rewards can be earned by keeping the group rules. Keep each activity short and focused.

You will notice that the session activities often switch from one kind of activity to another to help keep the pupils' interest, such as listening, looking, doing, playing a game and role play. This also helps if a pupil has difficulty with one skill, perhaps listening, as there are opportunities to learn in different ways.

Using tokens and rewards

You can use tokens, for example, counters or buttons, to reinforce appropriate behaviour, listening skills and keeping the group rules. These can be exchanged at the end of the session for a small reward. We found it worked well when we gave out four tokens during the session at the end of each activity, which could then be exchanged for a marshmallow at the end. It was surprising how consistently effective this small reward was as an incentive. Alternatively, you could give out raffle tickets and have a raffle at the end of the session, so that the more raffle tickets the pupil earns the more chance they have of winning.

Using a calming activity

If the group comes in unsettled, a quick calming activity such as slow breathing can help. This involves breathing in through the nose to a count of 3 and out through the mouth to a count of 7. The group can be challenged to see who can breathe out to 12, 15 and 20. The trick is not to hold the breath but to breathe out very gently. They can put the back of their hands near their mouth to feel the breath coming out very gently and slowly. By the time you have completed this activity, the group should be calm and quiet as they have been concentrating on their breathing.

Dealing with one group member who is being difficult to manage

Often peer pressure is enough to settle one difficult group member if the other members are 'on side'. However, if one member continues to be difficult, sometimes a quiet supportive word in between sessions can be enough to manage the situation. If you feel that the disruptive member is seeking attention, try to give them a special task during the next session, such as giving out equipment or deciding when tokens are earned. Sometimes using the disruptive member as an ally can be more effective than confronting them. You need to use your skills to decide which course of action will work best.

Be organised and well prepared

The best thing you can do to prevent behaviour management issues in the group sessions, which has already been mentioned but is worth mentioning again, is to make sure that the group facilitator is well prepared and organised. This includes being on time for the group, making sure that they are familiar with what the particular session entails, and having all the materials and handouts ready and in order. Make sure that any equipment such as pens, scissors, glue and card are available. Don't forget, of course, any tokens and rewards that you need. Also be aware that how the group session goes is often very dependent on your mood that day. If you are feeling under the weather, you will either have to make a special effort throughout the duration of the group not to let it show, or ask your co-facilitator to take the lead for that particular session. Vulnerable pupils can often sense how committed the group leader is during the session and if they do not seem to have everything under control, pupils are unfortunately more likely to be unsettled. This may not lead to good outcomes for the session. However, if one of the pupils is under the weather, this is a good opportunity for the group leaders to model caring and supportive behaviour towards that group member.

Ending the group

Often, during the process of taking part in the group, close relationships may be formed between the group facilitator and group members and between the group members themselves. So it is important to have an appropriate and positive ending to the group. Depending on your context, you may decide to have a mini-celebration with a cake or other treat at the end. We found it worked well to ask the pupils to complete their evaluation sheets and when they had done so, to present certificates to the group members with a mini-presentation ceremony to recognise their hard work and contribution to the group. We also made up anger management workbooks for each group member containing all the handouts and worksheets they had completed during the programme and allowed them to decorate the covers of these workbooks.

Preparing the session materials

Before the group starts some preparation of materials is needed. When photocopying any sheets that the pupil has to write on, we suggest you make a couple of extra copies as some pupils get very distressed if they make a mistake on their sheet.

Session 1

- Photocopy or print handouts.

- Prepare sheets of smaller card by cutting a 1cm strip off the width and length of the A4 card.

- We suggest you laminate a copy of the firework model as this is used as an illustration throughout the course.

Session 2

- Photocopy or print the sheet of rules agreed on last week for each pupil.

- Photocopy or print a set of caveman faces and feelings for each pupil or pair of pupils ready to sort.

- Make up the feelings blog booklets for each pupil.

- Cut out the feelings bingo boards (which can be laminated if you wish).

- Cut out the feelings bingo words ready to pull out of an envelope and the blank squares with which to cover the words on the boards.

- Make sure you have your digital camera ready to take the self-esteem photos for next week.

Session 3

- Print copies of the photos taken of each pupil last week.

- Photocopy or print strengths and skills sheets.

Session 4

- Laminate pupils' strengths and skills work to hand back.

- Photocopy or print pictures of matches, a thermometer sheet, list of synonyms and anger graphs for each pupil.

- Photocopy or print the coloured pictures and using the puzzle template cut each one into puzzle pieces. Put one piece into an envelope with a copy of the picture on the envelope. Mix up all the other pieces and divide them among the envelopes ready for the cooperative puzzle exercise.

Session 5

- Make sure the cooperative puzzle envelopes are prepared as for last week's session.

- Do an internet image search for the visual illusions. We suggest you search for 'visual illusions' and then use Rubin's Vase, Young Girl–Old Woman, Rabbit–Duck, Eskimo–Indian and Horse–Frog, as these were the ones we found got the point across best.

- Photocopy handouts and anger logs.

- You will need a ruler and pen as props for the role play.

Session 6

- Make sure cooperative puzzles are prepared as before.

- Photocopy or print handouts.

Session 7

* Photocopy or print handouts.

* Reduce down one sheet for each pupil of the anger management strategies so that they can cut them out if they need to in order to stick them in the Chinese fortune teller.

* Prepare the squares of coloured card ready to make the Chinese fortune tellers.

Session 8

* Make sure that the cooperative puzzles are prepared as before.

* Print out pictures of the animal cards and laminate them if you do not have puppets to use.

* Photocopy worksheets and handouts.

After the group

* Prepare booklets of the pupils' work and/or certificates to present to them.

* Photocopy the pupils' post-intervention evaluation sheets.

ANGER
MANAGEMENT
Resource sessions

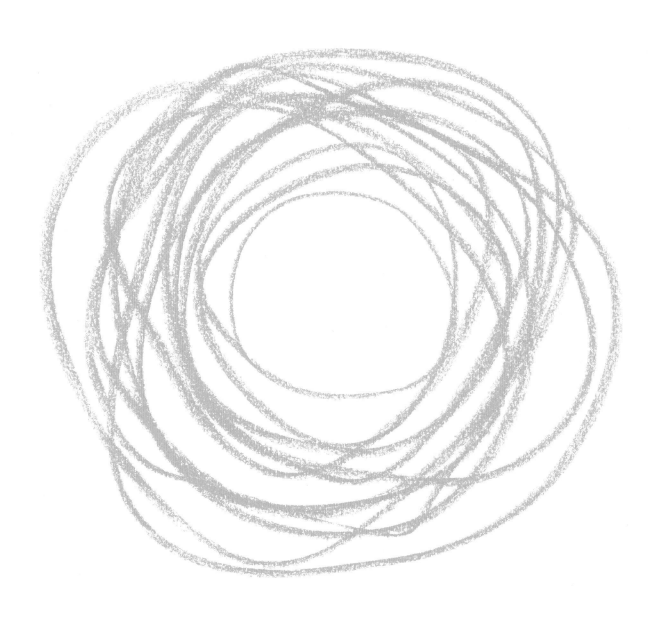

SESSION 1
Understanding anger

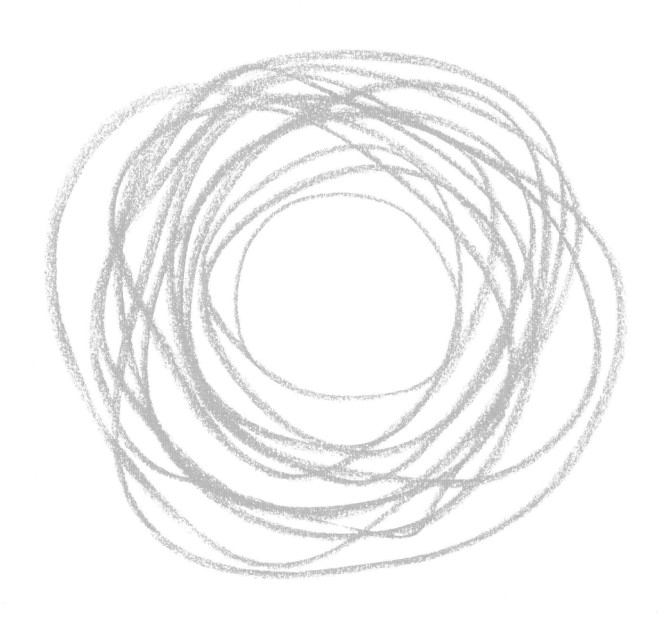

ANGER MANAGEMENT
Session 1
Understanding anger

Aims

- To understand and contribute to group rules for the sessions.

- To understand the fight/flight model of anger and its function, and that anger is a normal emotion.

- To think about the benefits of managing anger more effectively and the positive changes this will mean.

Resources

- Tokens and marshmallows (if needed)

- Caveman story

- Fight/flight picture sheet

- Two A4 sheets of coloured card or coloured paper (one slightly smaller than the other) for each pupil

- Spare coloured card or coloured paper

- Quick quiz

- Motivation box sheet

- Firework model

Start-up activities

- Introduce the group and its purpose, discuss group rules and ask what rules the group members think are important, for example:

  - Confidentiality.

  - Listen and take turns.

  - Respect each other.

- Write these up to bring back next week.

Understanding anger

- Read the caveman story and give out the fight/flight picture sheet.

- Ask for examples of when the fight/flight response can be helpful, for example, running a race; if someone is in danger and needs saving.

Increasing motivation to change

Move on to talk about times when the flight/fight being angry response has been unhelpful, for example, stops them doing well in school; stops them being in the school football team; getting into trouble with the police; upsetting family.

Making the motivation box

Pupils choose one large and one slightly smaller sheet of card. They then follow the instructions to make a box. Pupils reframe the statements about how angry responses adversely affect their lives to sentences of positive intent. For example:

If I could manage my anger …

… I would get on better with my friends.

… I would do well in school.

… I would stop getting into trouble.

They write these on coloured paper or card and put them in the box.

They can leave the box with the group leader or flatten it to take home and put somewhere to remind them of their intention to manage anger more appropriately and the likely positive consequences of doing so.

Plenary

Do the quick quiz.

Ending

Finish the session by showing the pupils the firework picture and talk about how we are going to look at different parts of anger to help us manage it differently.

Rewards

Hand out any rewards that have been earned.

The caveman story

Years and years ago, when we were cavemen and women and lived in caves, if a sabre-tooth tiger came up the hill to threaten us and our family there were only three things we could do. One was to play dead, which isn't a good idea as you'd probably get eaten. What two other things can you think of? (Fight or run away.)

Yes ,that's right, you could fight the tiger with your club or you could run away. These are instinctive reactions that have protected the human race so it has survived until today. Our bodies have been made so that when we sense danger our heart beats faster, thus pumping blood faster around our body so that the energy goes to our arms and legs and gives us extra strength to fight or to run away.

That's why when you feel angry you may notice you clench your fists or feel like punching or kicking.

There's something else that happens to us too. If the sabre-tooth tiger was approaching you could start thinking 'Um, shall I run away or fight? I do have my big club with me today but that looks like a particularly fierce sabre-tooth tiger. On the other hand, there is a tree over there that I could climb if I could run fast enough, and I am quite a fast runner.' What is likely to have happened by the time you had thought all that?

Yes, you would probably be tiger dinner by then. So something else happens when we feel threatened and get angry … the thinking part of our brain switches off. This is another thing that protected us. If we didn't think we just reacted quickly to the danger, we were more likely to survive.

Parts of our brains are the same as they were all those thousands of years ago. However, now there are no sabre-tooth tigers roaming around, but if someone threatens us, or our family, or even if we just feel not safe or OK, we have the same instincts to fight or run away. This is what happens to our bodies when we get angry.

As there are no sabre-tooth tigers to fight we have to learn ways of managing our feelings so that no one, including ourselves, ends up being hurt.

What makes us angry?

When our bodies sense danger, our blood rushes to our arms and legs to give us extra energy to fight the danger or run away from it.

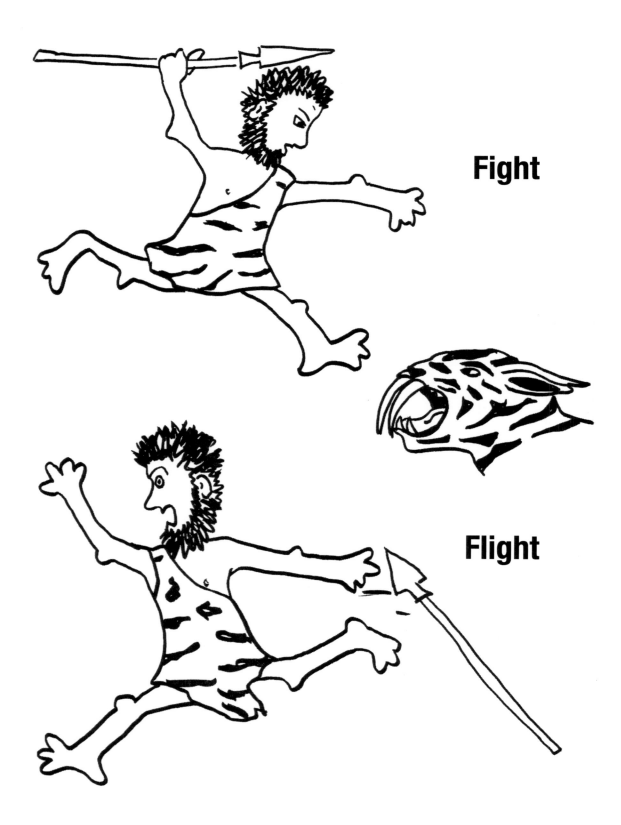

Fight

Flight

Quick quiz

1   Name one of our group rules.

2   What two things can we do when we are in danger?

3   Name one good thing anger can help us to do.

4   Name one bad thing anger can lead us to do.

5   Say one thing that will be better about your life if you can manage your anger better.

The Firework Model

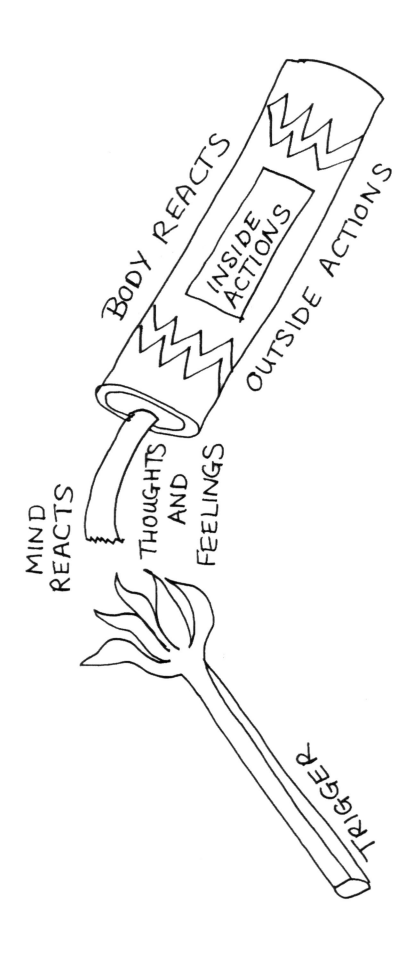

How to make a Motivation Box

Take a rectangle of stiff paper.

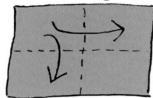 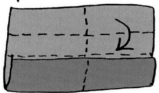

Fold from bottom to top and unfold it then fold side to side and unfold it.

Fold both the long edges to the middle. Crease and then unfold them.

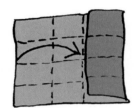 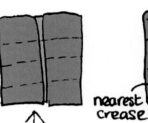

Fold both the short edges to the middle crease and leave them there.

Fold in all the corners so they meet the nearest crease.

nearest crease

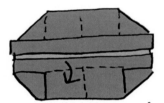 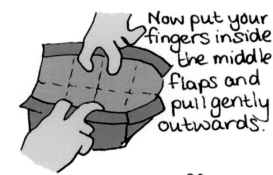

Fold back the edges in the middle so they overlap the corners you just made.

Now put your fingers inside the middle flaps and pull gently outwards.

Now pinch the corners to make your box stand upright.

Take 1cm strip off the long side and short side of another rectangle of stiff paper. make a second box. The larger box will fit over the smaller to make a lid.

ANGER MANAGEMENT
Session 1
Understanding anger

Teacher's feedback sheet

In this session the pupils learned:

* the fight/flight model of anger

* the function of anger as a survival instinct

* that anger is a normal emotion.

They thought about the benefits of being able to manage anger more effectively.

This is important because if they have a better understanding of anger and how it functions, it will help them to manage their anger safely.

You can support the pupils' learning by:

* giving them an opportunity to share what they have learned (either with you or with the rest of the class)

* relating the above ideas to any real-life examples at an appropriate time (not while the pupil is angry).

ANGER MANAGEMENT
Session 1
Understanding anger

Parent's/carer's feedback sheet

In this session your child learned:

* the fight/flight model of anger

* the function of anger as a survival instinct

* that anger is a normal emotion.

They thought about the benefits of being able to manage their anger more effectively.

This is important because if they have a better understanding of anger and how it functions, it will help them to manage their anger safely.

You can support your child's learning by:

* showing an interest in the course and giving them an opportunity to share what they have learned if they are willing to do so

* giving praise and encouragement to your child for participating in the groupwork and giving examples of how it will help them to be able to manage their anger better.

SESSION 2
Understanding feelings

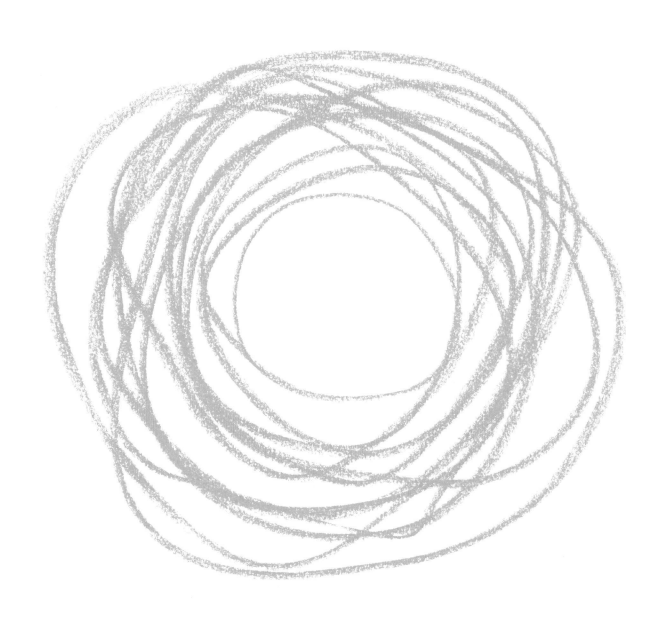

ANGER MANAGEMENT
Session 2
Understanding feelings

Aims

- To understand group rules for the sessions.
- To demonstrate understanding of 'feeling' words.

Resources

- Tokens and rewards
- Written sheet of rules (one per pupil) which were agreed last session
- Caveman faces with feeling labels
- Feelings bingo
- Feelings blog
- Camera

Recap group rules

Hand out copies of the rules agreed last week and ask pupils to sign them. Discuss how tokens can be earned by following the rules throughout the session.

Feelings sort

Sort feelings labels under two headings: 'good feelings' and 'uncomfortable feelings'.

Feelings bingo

Give each pupil a bingo board and some small squares of paper with which to cover up the words on their card. The group leader has a set of cards to match the emotions on the boards, and chooses one of the cards at random. The pupils can cover up the word on their board when they have been able to say something about the emotion depicted (for example, when they felt or might feel like this). 'Bingo' is called when a pupil completes their board.

Photos

Take a photo of each pupil to use on the self-esteem sheet next week. This can be a fun activity – who can make the 'coolest' pose? Be sure to let pupils know that they can delete pictures of themselves that they are not happy with.

Plenary

Put all the bingo cards in an envelope, then pull out one card at a time and mime the emotion. The first pupil to guess the word gets the card and each pupil's cards are totalled at the end to find the winner.

Or

Each pupil slaps their legs with the palms of their hands and then claps to a regular rhythm. On each clap, each pupil in turn must say the name of a feeling. If they hesitate, miss the beat or repeat a feeling that has already been used they are out. The winner is the last person left in. Those out first can listen out for repetition.

Follow-up activity

Hand out a feelings blog for pupils to complete between sessions.

Rewards

Hand out any rewards that have been earned.

Feelings bingo

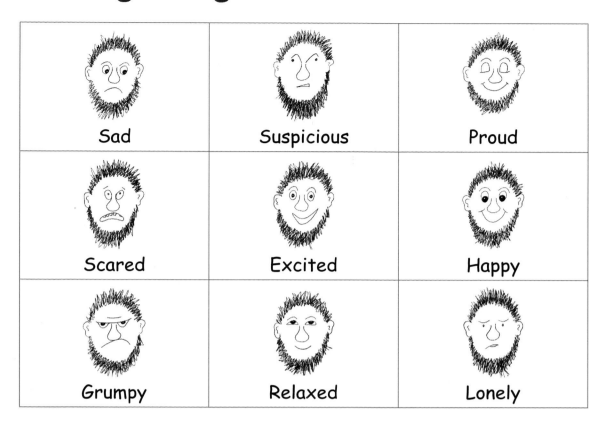

Sad	Suspicious	Proud
Scared	Excited	Happy
Grumpy	Relaxed	Lonely

Feelings bingo

Suspicious	Surprised	Tired
Proud	Thoughtful	Excited
Angry	Scared	Pleased

Feelings bingo

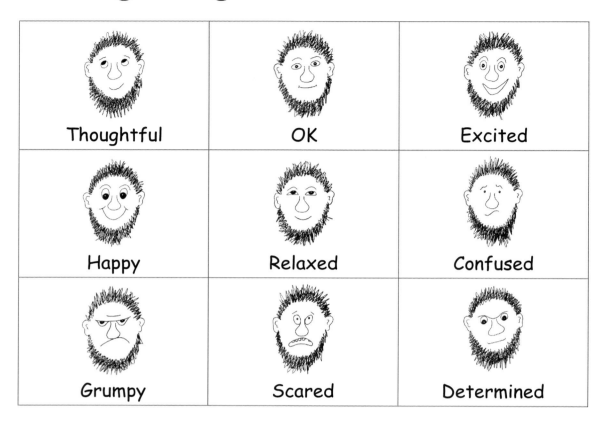

Thoughtful	OK	Excited
Happy	Relaxed	Confused
Grumpy	Scared	Determined

Feelings bingo

Angry	Frustrated	Determined
Tired	Surprised	Innocent
OK	Pleased	Satisfied

Feelings bingo

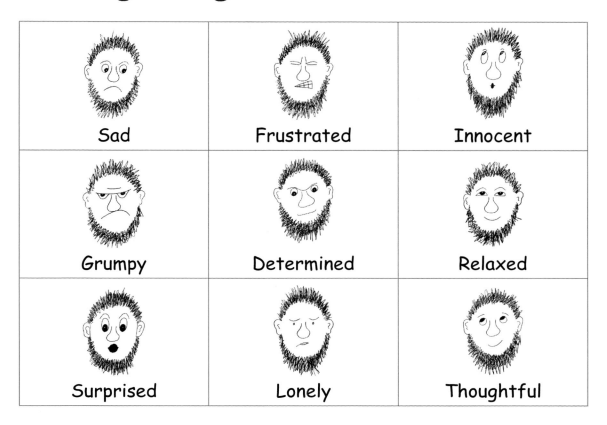

Sad	Frustrated	Innocent
Grumpy	Determined	Relaxed
Surprised	Lonely	Thoughtful

Feelings bingo

Innocent	Relaxed	Angry
Proud	Confused	Satisfied
Scared	Frustrated	Tired

Bingo cards

sad	suspicious	proud	scared
grumpy	excited	relaxed	happy
lonely	angry	surprised	thoughtful
tired	pleased	ok	confused
determined	frustrated	innocent	satisfied

Bingo cards

sad	suspicious	proud	scared
grumpy	excited	relaxed	happy
lonely	angry	surprised	thoughtful
tired	pleased	ok	confused
determined	frustrated	innocent	satisfied

Feelings labels

Uncomfortable feelings

Sad	Suspicious	Scared
Grumpy	Lonely	Tired
Angry	Confused	Frustrated

Feelings labels

Good feelings

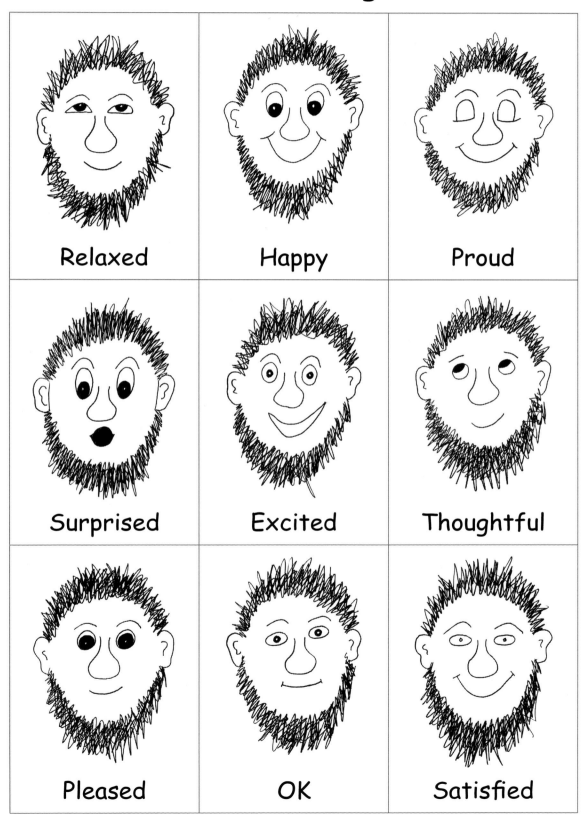

Relaxed	Happy	Proud
Surprised	Excited	Thoughtful
Pleased	OK	Satisfied

My feelings blog

Monday

Tuesday

Thursday

Wednesday

Friday

Date ▪▪▪▪▪▪▪▪▪▪▪▪▪▪▪▪▪▪▪▪▪▪▪ Date ....

How I felt today

Good Feelings

Surprised	Relaxed
Happy	OK
Excited	Thoughtful
Proud	Pleased

Uncomfortable Feelings

Angry	Sad
Tired	Lonely
Frustrated	Confused
Grumpy	Scared

Why did you feel that way?

Date ....

How I felt today

Uncomfortable Feelings

Angry	Sad
Tired	Lonely
Frustrated	Confused
Grumpy	Scared

Good Feelings

Surprised	Relaxed
Happy	OK
Excited	Thoughtful
Proud	Pleased

Why did you feel that way?

ANGER MANAGEMENT
Session 2
Understanding feelings

Teacher's feedback sheet

In this session the pupils learned:

- to explore feelings by sorting feeling words into good feelings and uncomfortable feelings.

They also gave examples of when they might experience different feelings.

This is important because anger is often a secondary emotion, and if a young person can name and express how they feel it will help them to manage feelings like anger more effectively.

You can support the pupils' learning by:

- reminding pupils to fill in the feelings blog they have been given to complete at the end of each day on how they felt and why. The completed 'blog' should be brought to the next session.

ANGER MANAGEMENT
Session 2
Understanding feelings

Parent's/carer's feedback sheet

In this session your child learned:

* to explore feelings by sorting feeling words into good feelings and uncomfortable feelings.

They also gave examples of when they might experience different feelings.

This is important because anger is often a secondary emotion, and if a young person can name and express how they feel it will help them to manage feelings like anger more effectively.

You can support your child's learning by:

* modelling the use of feeling words yourself in an appropriate context, for example, 'I was annoyed that it rained today and I got soaking wet' or 'I was angry my boss made me work late but it cheered me up hearing how well you had done at school today'

* reminding your child to fill in their 'feelings blog' at school ready for next week's session.

SESSION 3
Self-esteem

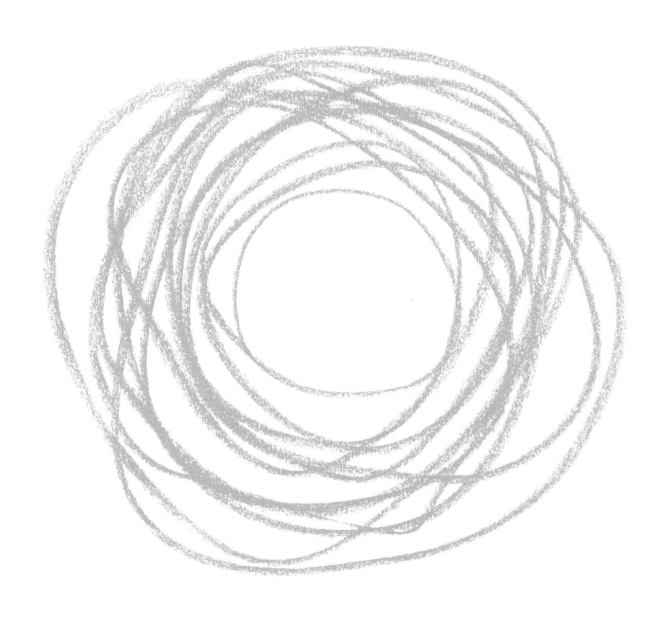

ANGER MANAGEMENT
Session 3
Self-esteem

Aims

- To identify each pupil's strengths and skills.
- To enable the pupils to have the resources necessary to change.
- To increase pupils' self-esteem and feeling of self-worth.
- To enable the pupils to be able to pay a compliment to another person.

Resources

- Group rules
- Tokens and rewards if needed
- Photos taken the previous week
- Strengths and skills blank sheets
- Strength cards
- Ball of string
- Glue and scissors

Recap group rules

- Confidentiality; listen and take turns; be kind.
- Reminder of how tokens and rewards can be earned.

Start-up activities

Review – each person chooses two examples to share from the blog they kept over the past week:

- a day that did not go well
- a good day.

Identifying own strengths and skills

- Pupils choose a photo or image of themselves, cut round it and stick it in the centre of their strengths and skills sheet.
- Lay out strengths and skills cards, then allow each pupil to pick six that are important to them and write them on the sheet.
- Help anyone struggling with this and give evidence to support suggestions, for example, 'I think you are *helpful* – remember how you put away the feeling words for me last week?'

Circle round

- In turn each pupil thinks of a positive quality they admire in each other (see suggestion above).

- The pupil adds each of the group's suggestions to their strengths and skills sheet, adding more boxes if necessary.

- The leader takes the sheet to type up and laminate for the pupil.

Plenary

The group sit in a circle. One person holds the end of a ball of string and passes the rest of the ball to another person, paying them a compliment as they do so, using the pupil's identified strengths and skills to do this. The next person holds the string tight and passes the rest of the ball to another person, paying them a compliment, so creating a criss-cross web of string between the pupils in the circle.

Follow-up activity

The pupils practise complimenting others over the next week.

Rewards

Hand out tokens and rewards that have been earned.

My strengths and skills

ANGER MANAGEMENT
Session 3
Self-esteem

Teacher's feedback sheet

In this session the pupils:

- identified their own strengths and skills

- were helped to recognise that they have the resources to make positive changes

- experienced being able to give and receive positive comments.

This is important because, unless the pupil knows what their strengths and skills are, and also knows that others believe in them, they will not be able to believe that they can make positive changes in their behaviour.

How the pupils' learning can be supported:

- Comment on any positive characteristics, strengths and skills you notice in the pupils during the week, always backing up your comments with examples of behaviour that demonstrate this. For example, 'Tom, I noticed how determined you were in gym today to climb to the top of the ropes, you just didn't give up.'

ANGER MANAGEMENT
Session 3
Self-esteem

Parent's/carer's feedback sheet

In this session your child:

* identified their own strengths and skills

* was helped to recognise that they have the resources to make positive changes

* experienced being able to give and receive positive comments.

This is important because, unless your child knows what their strengths and skills are, and also knows that others believe in them, they will not be able to believe that they can make positive changes in their behaviour.

You can support your child's learning by:

* commenting on your child's positive characteristics, strengths and skills as you notice them, always backing up your comments with examples of behaviour that demonstrate this (eg, 'Tom, I noticed how generous you were, sharing your sweets with your brother')

* allowing your child the opportunity to do things for other people that will lead to positive feedback (eg, if your child likes cooking, allowing them to make some cakes to share with family or friends).

SESSION 4
Triggers and fuses

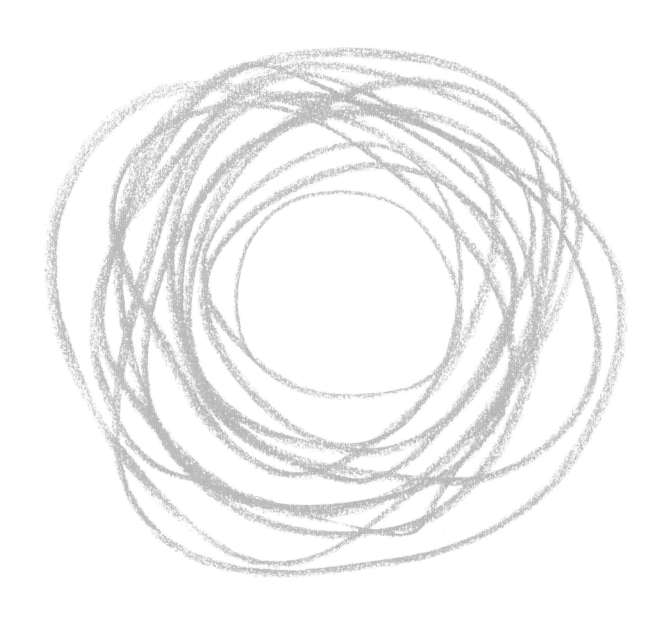

ANGER MANAGEMENT
Session 4
Triggers and fuses

Aims

- To acknowledge that everyone experiences strong feelings.
- To introduce the firework model and explore the range of triggers that can lead to angry feelings.

Resources

- Rewards and tokens if needed
- Firework model (Session 1)
- Pictures of matches
- List of synonyms for anger
- Cooperative puzzle (see CD for Puzzle Template)
- Anger graph
- Anger thermometer sheet

Recap group rules

- Confidentiality; listen and take turns; be kind.
- Reminder of how tokens and rewards can be earned.

Start-up activities

Cooperative picture puzzles – pupils are given one envelope each. Each envelope has a different picture on it. Inside the envelope are some jigsaw pieces which make up the picture. However, only one of the pieces matches the picture on the envelope. The other pieces belong to the other group members. The group must complete their own jigsaw following these rules:

- Work in silence.
- Give pieces away to others.
- Do not ask for, signal about or take pieces away from others.

Anger – a normal reaction

Reinforce the concept that anger is a normal emotion experienced by everyone. Anger may be an appropriate response in some situations; think of examples. The challenge is to stay safe when angry, and to keep others safe too.

Firework model

Look at the firework model, considering each part briefly. Talk about the trigger being the things that lead us to feel angry. Those angry feelings usually arise because we feel threatened in some way (not necessarily physically; it is often about looking or feeling stupid).

Once the angry feelings start, it is as if a fuse is burning. Some people have very short fuses and react quickly. Others have longer fuses and may simmer for a while before blowing up.

The firework represents us – if we don't stop the fuse burning, we will eventually have some kind of explosion.

Triggers and matches

Pupils think about personal triggers and write them on the pictures of matches. They can share these with the group and stick them on the firework poster.

Anger word list

List the range of words that come to mind when we describe anger. Using the anger thermometer sheet, cut up the anger synonyms and order, that is scale the words alongside according to level of intensity (ie from frustrated to furious).

Plenary

Name one trigger for your anger that makes you feel frustrated and one that makes you feel furious.

Follow-up activity

Hand out anger graphs for pupils to track the intensity of anger feelings over the day. The graph can be completed each day over the following week.

Rewards

Hand out tokens and rewards that have been earned.

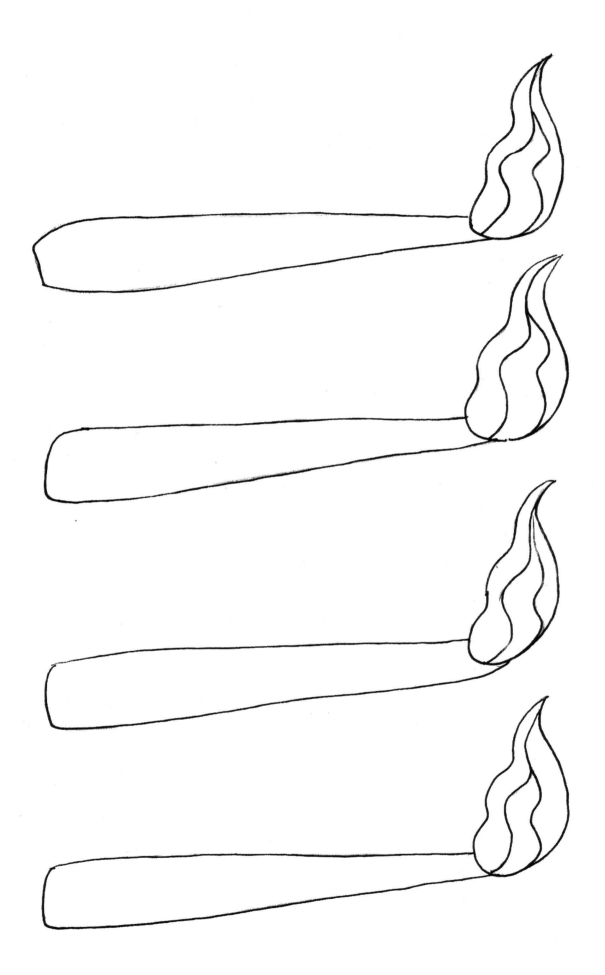

Anger thermometer

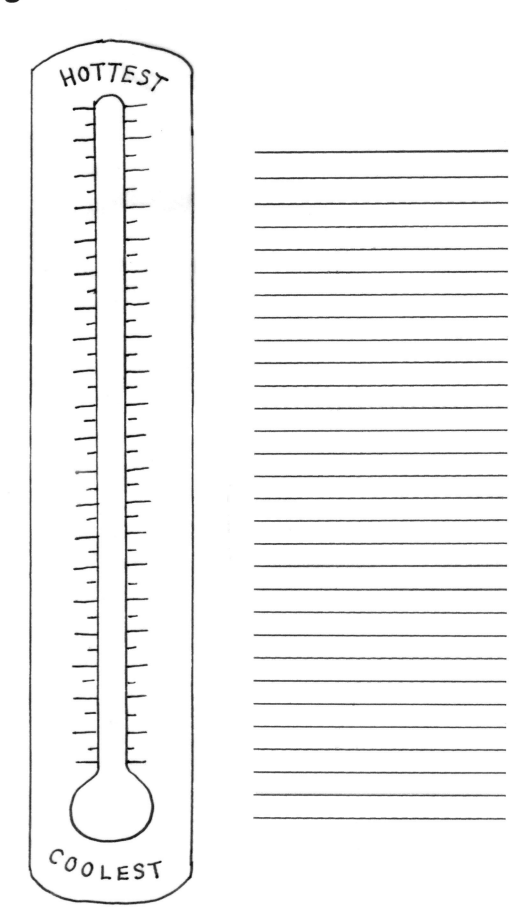

Anger synonyms

annoyed	seething
frustrated	heated
angry	provoked
cross	raging
mad	put out
fuming	snappy
furious	bothered
livid	grumpy
irritated	huffy
wound up	steaming
peeved	ranting
bad tempered	miffed

Anger Graph

Fill in the graph each day to show how angry you felt. 0 = cool as ice, 5 = hot explosions.

Include some labels to show why you felt angry.

Name: ....

MONDAY	Date						
5							
4							
3							
2							
1							
0							
	Before school	Lesson 1	Break	Lesson 2	Lunch	Lesson 3	After school

How well I managed my anger today ⎯10

TUESDAY	Date						
5							
4							
3							
2							
1							
0							
	Before school	Lesson 1	Break	Lesson 2	Lunch	Lesson 3	After school

How well I managed my anger today ⎯10

WEDNESDAY

	Before school	Lesson 1	Break	Lesson 2	Lunch	Lesson 3	After school	How well I managed my anger today $\frac{}{10}$
Date								
5								
4								
3								
2								
1								
0								

THURSDAY

	Before school	Lesson 1	Break	Lesson 2	Lunch	Lesson 3	After school	How well I managed my anger today $\frac{}{10}$
Date								
5								
4								
3								
2								
1								
0								

FRIDAY

	Before school	Lesson 1	Break	Lesson 2	Lunch	Lesson 3	After school	How well I managed my anger today $\frac{}{10}$
Date								
5								
4								
3								
2								
1								
0								

ANGER MANAGEMENT
Session 4
Triggers and fuses

Teacher's feedback sheet

In this session the pupils used a firework model to:

- think about anger as a feeling

- rate anger words according to their level of intensity

- learn what their own anger-triggers are.

This is important because pupils need to be aware of what the triggers for their anger are and how these light their fuse. They also need to be able to recognise when they start getting angry at an early stage so that they can do something about it before it builds up.

You can support the pupils' learning by:

- reminding the pupils to fill in the anger graph they have been given to track the intensity of angry feelings each day for a week; they should bring these completed sheets to the next session

- reflecting back if you notice that a pupil is out of sorts or irritable and supporting them by giving them opportunities to manage this before it increases to anger; for instance, do they need a snack or drink break or to change their activity or to move away from someone who is annoying them?

ANGER MANAGEMENT
Session 4
Triggers and fuses

Parent's/carer's feedback sheet

In this session your child used a firework model to:

* think about anger as a feeling

* rate anger words according to their level of intensity

* learn what their own anger triggers are.

This is important because they need to be aware of what the triggers for their anger are and how these light their fuse. They also need to be able to recognise when they start getting angry at an early stage so that they can do something about it before it builds up.

You can support your child's learning by:

* reminding them to complete their anger graphs in school to bring to the next session

* noticing when they are out of sorts or irritable and supporting them by giving them opportunities to manage this before it increases to anger; for instance, do they need a snack or drink break or to change their activity or to move away from someone who is annoying them?

SESSION 5
Learning to think differently

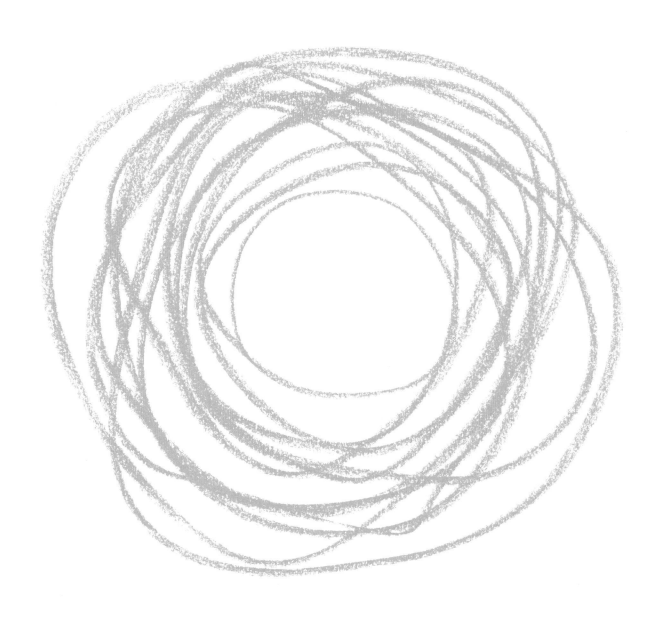

ANGER MANAGEMENT
Session 5
Learning to think differently

Aim

- To recognise different emotional states and the kinds of thoughts that power up or defuse anger.

Resources

- Tokens and rewards if needed
- Firework model
- Visual illusions
- Role plays
- 'Thinking differently' story
- Scenario and thought cards
- Anger log
- Cooperative puzzles (from Session 4)

Recap group rules

- Confidentiality; listen and take turns; be kind.
- Reminder of how tokens and rewards can be earned.

Start-up activities

Cooperative picture puzzles – pupils are given one envelope each. Each envelope has a different picture on it. Inside the envelope are some jigsaw pieces which make up the picture. However, only one of the pieces matches the picture on the envelope. The other pieces belong to the other group members. The group must complete their own jigsaw following these rules:

- Work in silence.
- Give pieces away to others.
- Do not ask for, signal about or take pieces away from others.

Review

Review the anger graphs. How angry did pupils feel? When did they feel most angry and when did they feel least angry? Look for any patterns and discuss.

Firework model

Last session's focus was the trigger. Today's is the fuse, particularly on how thoughts can power up or defuse anger.

Seeing things differently – visual illusions

Show the pictures one by one, asking pupils what they see. After looking at the illusions, reflect on the fact that everyone looked at the same pictures, but what they saw varied. The same can be true of events.

Facilitator reads the 'Thinking differently' story.

Role play

Using the role play script the group facilitator asks a pupil to act out the role play with them. This further illustrates how situations can be seen in different ways, and that it is what we think about the situation rather than the situation itself that causes us to feel or act a certain way.

The power of thoughts

When something happens to trigger angry feelings, the way we think about it will affect what we do. Changing the way we think about it can give us more time (lengthen the fuse) to consider how we will choose to act.

Look together at the scenario cards. Imagine the scenario has happened to you. Pick two thought cards that show the two different ways that you could think about the scenario. Which thought would be most likely to lead you to feel angry? Which thought would be most likely to 'lengthen your fuse'? It might be helpful to do this in pairs. Pupils could colour code the different thoughts or sort them under headings. They could then role play the scenarios and the group could identify which type of thought was role played: a 'helpful thought' that would lengthen their fuse or an 'unhelpful thought' that might lead to anger.

Plenary

Can you think of other ways you might think about the incidents above that would lengthen your fuse?

Follow-up activity

Pupils begin to keep a record of times when angry feelings occur. They can use the anger log to identify the trigger, thoughts and feelings that powered up or defused the situation, and the consequent actions (did the firework explode or remain intact)?

Rewards

Hand out tokens and rewards that have been earned.

Thinking differently

(To be read by group facilitator)

Imagine you have been shopping for your mum. You are really pleased because you managed to get everything she wanted, including some eggs which you have remembered to put carefully at the top of your carrier bag so that they don't get squashed and broken. Suddenly, as you are walking home and glancing down at the shopping, someone barges into you so that you lose your grip on the shopping bag and the eggs slip out on to the ground and smash. You turn around to speak to the person who has knocked into you.

What are you thinking? (The stupid idiot?)

How are you feeling? (Angry?)

Yes, you are probably feeling really angry, but when you look back you see that the person who knocked into you is a little old lady using a white stick as she is unable to see.

Now what are you thinking? (She couldn't help it – she couldn't see?)

How are you feeling now? Do you feel as angry as you did before? (Well, no, because it wasn't her fault – she couldn't help it she couldn't see.)

But your mum's eggs are still broken; the situation is still the same. It is the way you are thinking that is different, and that has changed the way you feel.

This story shows that it is not what happens to you that makes you feel angry, it is how you think about it. Therefore, if you can change the way you think about a situation, you can stop yourself from feeling so angry about that situation.

Role plays

Example 1

Persons A and B

Prop = decorative ruler or pencil case

Scene 1

A picks up ruler and looks at it.

B (angrily) 'Hey, what are you doing? Give that back to me!' (snatches ruler back)

Scene 2

A picks up ruler and looks at it.

B (smiling) 'Do you like that? My mum gave it me for Christmas – it's nice, isn't it?'

Ask the pupils:

How did B respond in the first scene? (He was shouting.)

Why? (B was angry.)

What was B thinking? (He thought A was stealing his ruler.)

So what was different about the two scenes? A did exactly the same thing – just looked at the ruler – yet the first time B got really angry and the second time B was pleased and calm. (It was what B was thinking that was different.)

Example 2

Persons A and B

Prop = a pen

Scene 1

B walks towards the door and drops the pen without seeming to notice.

A calls out B's name, 'B!' (intending to let them know they have dropped their pen). However, before they can say this B turns around and shouts angrily.

'What! What do you want now? You're always picking on me. Well go on, what have I done now?'

B 'You've dropped your pen.'

Scene 2

B walks towards the door and drops the pen without seeming to notice.

A calls out B's name, 'B!' (intending to let them know they have dropped their pen).

B turns round and asks 'Yes?'

A says 'You've dropped your pen.'

B 'Oh, thank you.'

Ask the pupils:

How did B respond in the first scene? (He was shouting.)

Why? (B was angry.)

What was B thinking? (He thought A was going to tell him off for something or have a go at him.)

So what was different about the two scenes? A did exactly the same thing – just called B's name – yet the first time B got really angry and the second time B was pleased and calm. (It was what B was thinking that was different.)

So can you see that it is not what happens that makes someone angry but what they think about the situation.

Scenario card

Sarah's friend borrowed her new CD a month ago. Sarah keeps asking for it back but her friend has still not given it to her.

She always takes my stuff. She probably wants to keep it and never give it back.

She is a very forgetful person. Maybe she keeps forgetting to give it back.

Scenario card

Scenario card

In an English lesson Emily's best friend does not talk to her.

She does not want to be my friend.

I know my friend had a bad argument at home today. She might be trying to think about what has happened.

Scenario card

Scenario card

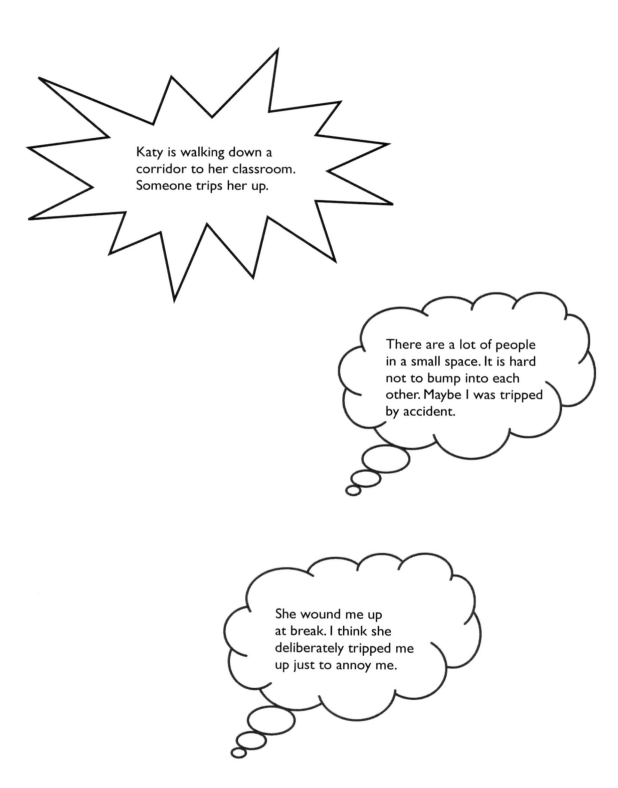

Katy is walking down a corridor to her classroom. Someone trips her up.

There are a lot of people in a small space. It is hard not to bump into each other. Maybe I was tripped by accident.

She wound me up at break. I think she deliberately tripped me up just to annoy me.

Scenario card

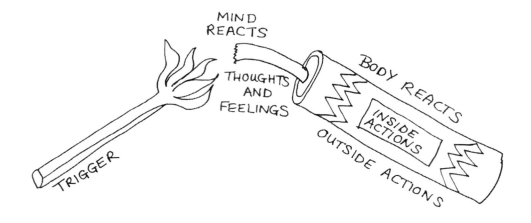

My anger log

Feeling angry is OK, what really matters is how you show it. Every day think of an incident that happened. It could be something that went well or it could be something that you wish you had handled differently. Think about what happens to a firework and see if you can manage to make your fuse longer and stay calm rather than having an explosion!

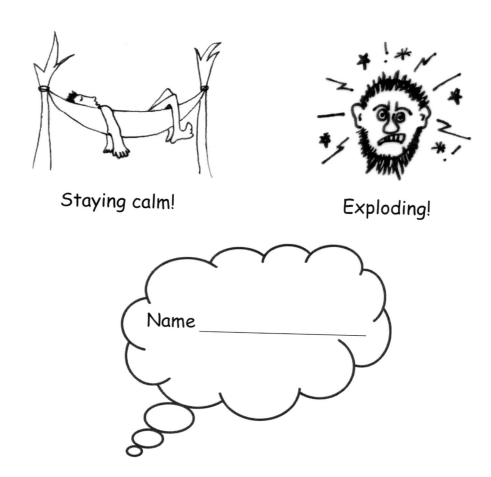

Staying calm!

Exploding!

Name _____

Try to think of an incident a day that went well and one where you think you could have handled matters better. Write or draw what you thought and what happened.

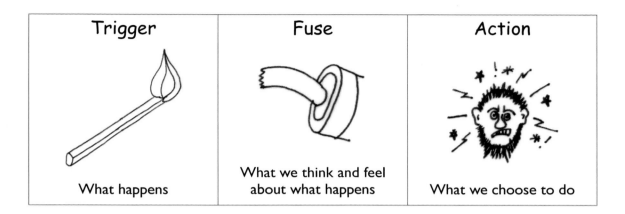

Trigger	Fuse	Action
What happens	What we think and feel about what happens	What we choose to do

Day 1

Trigger	Fuse	Action
1		
2		

Day 2

	Trigger	Fuse	Action
1			
2			

Day 3

	Trigger	Fuse	Action
1			
2			

Day 4

	Trigger	Fuse	Action
1			
2			

Day 5

	Trigger	Fuse	Action
1			
2			

ANGER MANAGEMENT
Session 5
Learning to think differently

Teacher's feedback sheet

Using the firework model again, in this session the pupils learned:

- that there are different ways of viewing situations

- that it is their thoughts about a situation that determine how they might react, not the situation itself.

This is important because bad things can always happen in life and there will always be people who may wind the pupil up. Neither you nor the pupil can change that, but they can change the way they view or think about situations so that they don't feel so angry about them.

You can support the pupils' learning by:

- reminding the pupils to fill in the anger log they have been given to record times when they feel angry, what their thoughts and feelings were and consequent actions

- discussing with the pupils whether their thoughts defused or ignited their anger.

- reminding the pupils to bring their completed sheets to the next session.

ANGER MANAGEMENT
Session 5
Learning to think differently

Parent's/carer's feedback sheet

Using the firework model again, in this session your child learned:

- that there are different ways of viewing situations

- that it is their thoughts about a situation that determine how they might react, not the situation itself.

This is important because bad things can always happen in life and there will always be people who may wind your child up. Neither you nor your child can change that, but they can change the way they view or think about situations so that they don't feel so angry about them.

You can support your child's learning by:

- reminding your child to fill in their anger logs at school to bring to the next session

- discussing with them examples of how changing the way you think can change the way you feel. (Eg 'I could feel angry that your brother broke your computer game, but I know that he really liked playing with it too so it must have been an accident.')

SESSION 6
Physiology and relaxation

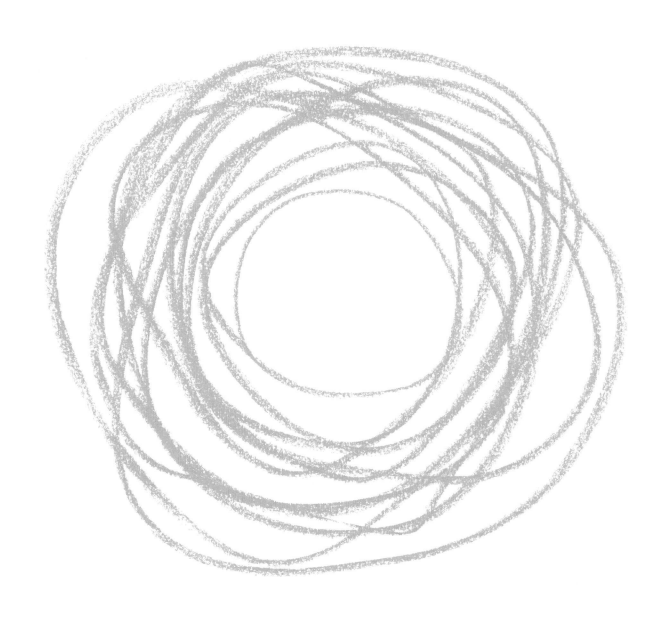

ANGER MANAGEMENT
Session 6
Physiology and relaxation

Aim

- To recognise the physical feelings that accompany anger and to begin to identify some calming strategies.

Resources

- Tokens and rewards if needed
- Firework model
- 'Where do I feel anger in my body?' sheet
- Breathing log
- 'The News' interview sheet
- Cooperative puzzles

Recap group rules

- Confidentiality; listen and take turns; be kind.
- Reminder of how tokens and rewards can be earned.

Start-up activities

Cooperative picture puzzles – pupils are given one envelope each. Each envelope has a different picture on it. Inside the envelope are some jigsaw pieces which make up the picture. However, only one of the pieces matches the picture on the envelope. The other pieces belong to the other group members. The group must complete their own jigsaw following these rules:

- Work in silence.
- Give pieces away to others.
- Do not ask for, signal about or take pieces away from others.

Review

Review anger logs. Ask each pupil to identify a trigger, fuse thought and action.

Firework model

Last session's focus was the fuse. This week we are looking at the explosive cylinder and physical feelings.

Physical signals

Anger can be accompanied by a variety of physical feelings or signals. These can be useful early warning signals to use if we become more aware of what typically happens in our own bodies.

Take a few deep breaths and remember an experience that made you very angry. Where did you feel anger in your body?

Pupils complete the 'Where do I feel anger in my body?' sheet.

Alternative activity

Pupils draw round each other on a giant sheet of paper and label where they feel anger.

Breathing techniques

Ask pupils to breathe in through their nose to the count of 3 and then breathe out through their mouth to the count of 7. Challenge the pupils to see how long they can manage (10, then 15, then 20). Use your fingers to count the seconds, as it gives the pupil something to focus on as they concentrate on their deep breathing.

Tell them the trick is not to hold their breath but to breathe out in a slow controlled way. Pupils can put the backs of their hands in front of their mouths to feel the breath coming out slowly and softly.

Relaxation techniques

1   Tensing and relaxing muscles

Ask the pupils to sit comfortably, then to tense and relax their muscles from their head down starting with their face. See who can make the silliest face. Then tense and relax their shoulders, then put their arms out straight in front of them, clench their fists and tense their arms, then relax them.

Check arms by lifting the wrist a couple of inches and seeing if it falls back down. Demonstrate this yourself if necessary. Then move on to tensing and relaxing bottoms, legs and feet.

2   The 3,2,1 mindfulness exercise

Ask the pupils to sit comfortably and then ask them to concentrate and say three things they can see, then three things they can hear and then three things they can feel. Then two things they can see, hear and feel and then one thing they can see, hear, and feel.

Plenary

Pupils interview someone else in the group recording their answers on the 'News' interview sheet.

Follow-up activity

Practise using the breathing technique over the next week. Note in the breathing log the times you managed to use the technique. What number did you get to?

Rewards

Hand out any rewards and tokens that have been earned.

Where do I feel anger in my body?

Breathing techniques

Breathe in through your nose to the count of 3 and then breathe out through your mouth to the count of 7. See whether you can manage 10, then 15, then 20. The trick is not to hold your breath but to breathe out very slowly. Use your fingers to count the seconds, as it gives you something to focus on as you concentrate on your deep breathing.

Days of the week	Where were you?	What number did you get to?
Monday		1 2 3 4 5 6 7 8 9 10 11 12 13 14 15 16 17 18 19 20
Tuesday		1 2 3 4 5 6 7 8 9 10 11 12 13 14 15 16 17 18 19 20
Wednesday		1 2 3 4 5 6 7 8 9 10 11 12 13 14 15 16 17 18 19 20
Thursday		1 2 3 4 5 6 7 8 9 10 11 12 13 14 15 16 17 18 19 20
Friday		1 2 3 4 5 6 7 8 9 10 11 12 13 14 15 16 17 18 19 20

You are a reporter who is interviewing one of the group. Ask them the following questions:

Name of the person you are interviewing:

_____

What happens to your body when you start to get angry?

_____

_____

_____

What could you do to try and relax and stay calm when people make you angry?

_____

_____

_____

Well done, star reporter! You have finished your report!

ANGER MANAGEMENT
Session 6
Physiology and relaxation

Teacher's feedback sheet

In this session the pupils learned:

- where in their body they feel anger and how to recognise early warning signs

- some breathing and relaxation techniques.

This is important because, unless the pupil can recognise how their body is feeling, they won't know the warning signs of anger in time to be able to do anything about it.

You can support the pupils' learning by:

- reminding the pupils to fill in the sheet they have been given to record their daily practice of breathing exercises; this completed sheet should be brought to the next session

- supporting the pupils to think about using relaxation techniques when they are beginning to feel under stress.

ANGER MANAGEMENT
Session 6
Physiology and relaxation

Parent's/carer's feedback sheet

In this session your child learned:

- where in their body they feel anger and how to recognise early warning signs

- some breathing and relaxation techniques.

This is important because, unless your child can recognise how their body is feeling, they won't know the warning signs of anger in time to be able to do anything about it.

You can support your child's learning by:

- reminding them to do their breathing and relaxation exercises and complete their record sheet to bring to the next session

- giving them an opportunity to share the techniques they have learned with you.

SESSION 7
Strategies to manage anger

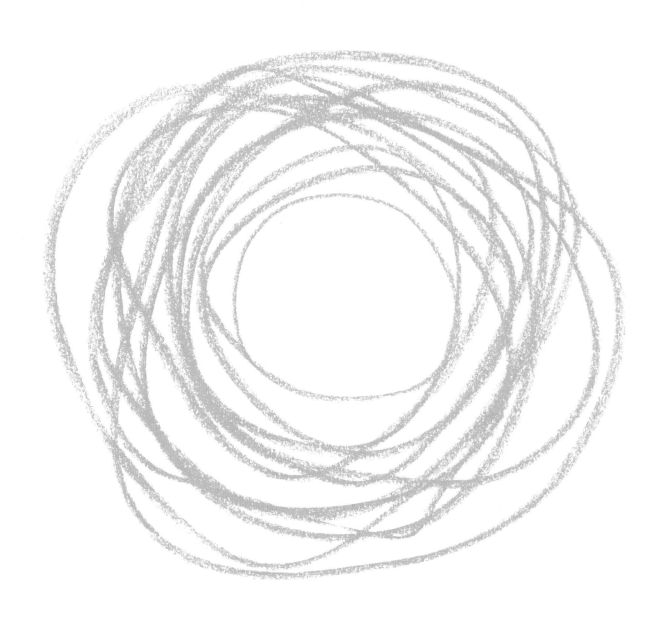

ANGER MANAGEMENT
Session 7
Strategies to manage anger

Aim

- To enable pupils to learn strategies that will help them to manage angry feelings appropriately.

Resources

- Group rules
- Tokens and rewards if needed
- Firework model
- List of strategies
- Leader's strategy information sheet
- Picture strategy list
- Coloured squares of thin card (20cm square)
- Fortune teller instruction sheet

Recap group rules

- Confidentiality; listen and take turns; be kind.
- Reminder of how tokens and rewards can be earned.

Start-up activities

Look at the pupils' breathing technique record sheets from last week. See how everyone got on.

Firework model

Look again at the firework model. Today we will think about ways to dampen the fuse so that we do not explode with anger.

Relaxing scene

Ask the pupils to imagine themselves in a peaceful, relaxing scene. For example, lying on the beach with the sea lapping at their toes. Ask the pupils how they feel. When could they and when would they use this strategy? Can they think of any other strategies?

Learning strategies

Go through the list of strategies. Explain each one in turn. Discuss which ones might work for them and in what context (eg classroom, playground, at home).

Choosing strategies

Ask the pupils to choose some strategies from the list to try during the coming week and plan how they will use them.

Show the pupils how to make a Chinese fortune teller and then copy, or cut and paste, their favourite eight strategies into the spaces under the numbered flaps.

Alternatively pupils can cut out three strategies from the picture sheet and paste them on to their sheet of strategies to try.

Plenary

Let the pupils try out their fortune tellers on each other.

Follow-up activity

Practise using their chosen strategies during the week. Choose an example to talk about next week.

Rewards

Hand out tokens and rewards that have been earned.

Anger management strategies

Think about incentives or goals you want to achieve.

Relax clenched muscles.

Breathe deeply and slowly.

Recite 7 x table in head.

Listen to music.

Find a special person to be with.

Have a special place to go.

Squeeze a stress ball.

Take some exercise (running, football).

Hide behind an imaginary shield of positive images.

Pretend to be somewhere else.

Recite the alphabet backwards till you become an expert at it and can impress everybody.

Talk yourself into feeling calm by challenging the angry thoughts.

Remove yourself from the situation as fast as you can.

Time out card.

Imagine the person who is making you angry is talking in a silly voice.

Get help for the situation that is making you angry.

Think about someone you love and what they would say.

Listen really carefully to the person who is making you angry and try to see their point of view.

Think whether there is a solution to the problem that could please everyone.

Think 'Is this worth the trouble?'

Draw a picture.

Write a letter.

Keep a diary.

Go to bed at a reasonable time.

Be honest about how you feel in a way that doesn't hurt anybody.

Think of something you are good at.

Think of your own ideas to try.

Anger management strategies

Group leader's information sheet

Think about incentives or goals you want to achieve.
(Perhaps your parents have promised you extra pocket money if you are good or you want to be allowed on that school trip.)

Relax clenched muscles.
(Tense and relax each muscle in turn and then relax them – see Session 6.)

Breathe deeply and slowly.
(Breathe in through the nose to 3 and out through the mouth to 7.)

Recite 7 times table in head.
(Counting in 10s is too easy – choose a times table that you have to concentrate on.)

Listen to music.
(What music do you like? When could you use this strategy?)

Find a special person to be with.
(Who would that person be if you were at home? In school? In the playground?)

Have a special place to go.
(Where could you use this strategy? Where would you go?)

Squeeze a stress ball.
(Where could you get one? Where would you keep it?)

Take some exercise (running, football).
(Where and when could you do this? What would you do?)

Hide behind an imaginary shield of positive images.
(Draw a shield, divide it into four, and then draw four things you are good at or that mean a lot to you; think of a motto; think of this shield if someone upsets you.)

Pretend to be somewhere else.
(Where would you be? – on a sandy beach, the waves lapping perhaps?)

Recite the alphabet backwards till you become an expert at it and can impress everybody.
(z, y, x, w, etc.)

Talk yourself into feeling calm by challenging the angry thoughts.
(Think, 'Its not my problem, it's theirs, I am not going to let them wind me up.')

Remove yourself from the situation as fast as you can.
(Just walk away or leave the room.)

Time out card.
(Arrange with your teacher to be able to leave the room and calm down outside for 60 seconds.)

Imagine the person who is making you angry is talking in a silly voice.
(Eg a high squeaky voice or a low rumbly voice.)

Get help for the situation that is making you angry.
(Speak to someone and see if they can help you change what's happening.)

Think about someone you love and what they would say.
(This could be your mum, dad, nan, grandad or even someone who has died.)

Listen really carefully to the person who is making you angry and try to see their point of view.
(Think what you would like to happen if you were in their position.)

Think whether there is a solution to the problem that could please everyone.
(Perhaps you'll find a suitable compromise.)

Think 'Is this worth the trouble?'
(Think about what negative consequences there would be if you react badly to the situation.)

Draw a picture.
(Draw something that will take your mind off the immediate issue.)

Write a letter.
(Write to the person who is causing you stress or to someone who you'd like to empathise with you.)

Keep a diary.
(The diary could be a record of all the situations you've been in and how you chose to react to them.)

Go to bed at a reasonable time.
(Getting more sleep will help you tolerate others.)

Be honest about how you feel in a way that doesn't hurt anybody.
(Explain what is upsetting you and what you'd like to change; use 'I' messages.)

Think of something you are good at.
(Eg when you played football and scored a winning goal.)

Think of your own ideas to try.
(Try them out and see which ones are helpful.)

Dampening the fuse and keeping calm – strategy list

Cut out the three ways that you most think would help you to stay calm.

Try walking away from the incident. If you walk away you can't hear what upsets you.	
Try using some extra energy. How about playing football with a friend?	
Use a catchphrase. Talk to yourself to keep yourself calm.	I am a cool person and nothing can upset me!
Pretend that you are somewhere else, like on holiday or in your bedroom.	

Clench and relax all the muscles in your body. Start from your head and work down to your toes.	
Listening to your favourite music can help you relax. It can be something loud or quiet – just as long as it makes you feel better!	
Try counting. If 10 is not enough, try counting in your head to 20 or even 30 if you need to.	**1, 2, 3, 4...**
Use the turtle technique. Imagine you have a shield that can protect you from anything.	
Try to relax. Sit down, close your eyes, take a deep breath in and let it out slowly.	

How to make a Chinese fortune teller

Make a square piece of paper by folding one corner of a rectangle piece to the adjacent side and then cutting off the small rectangle at the top.

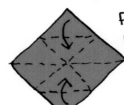

Fold the two opposite sides of the triangle together making a smaller triangle and then open up the paper (unfolding all the folds).

Fold a corner into the central point. Repeat with the other two corners. You'll end up with a square.

Flip the paper over and repeat the previous instruction. You'll end up with a smaller square.

Fold the square in half. Unfold and fold in half the other way.

Unfold and pull the four ends together, making a diamond-like shape. Pick up each of the four square flaps and put your fingers inside. You will be able to move the four parts around by using the thumb and index finger of each hand. Write four colours on the four flaps.

Flip it over and write 1-8 on the triangular flaps.

Then write 8 anger management strategies inside the flaps (underneath the numbers).

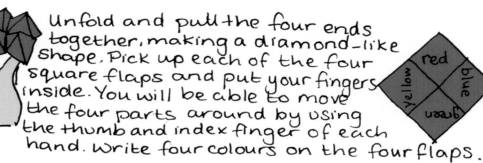

As you move the four parts open and shut ask someone to choose a colour and then a number until their second choice of number reveals a strategy to read out.

ANGER MANAGEMENT
Session 7
Strategies to manage anger

Teacher's feedback sheet

In this session the pupils learned:

* to look at different strategies to manage angry feelings

* which ones work for them and in what context (classroom, playground, etc)

* to develop an individual plan or strategy for managing anger.

This is important because the pupils need to have a plan of action ready to use if they feel themselves starting to get angry.

You can support the pupils' learning by:

* discussing with the pupils what strategies they plan to use and asking whether you can support them in any way

* if triggers occur, supporting pupils to use their strategy.

NB. Do not attempt to persuade a pupil to use their strategy in a situation where they are already at a high level of anger and beyond rational thinking. If an angry outburst occurs, discuss with the pupil at a different time, when they are calm, how they could be supported to use their strategy next time.

ANGER MANAGEMENT
Session 7
Strategies to manage anger

Parent's/carer's feedback sheet

In this session your child learned:

- to look at different strategies to manage angry feelings

- which strategies work for them and in what context (classroom, playground, home)

- to develop an individual plan or strategy for managing anger.

This is important because your child needs to have a plan of action ready to use if they feel themselves starting to get angry.

You can support your child's learning by:

- talking through your child's plan with them and asking them whether there is anything you can do to support them with it

- supporting them, if triggers occur, to use their strategy, as above.

NB. Do not attempt to persuade your child to use their strategy in a situation where they are already at a high level of anger and beyond rational thinking. If an angry outburst occurs, discuss with your child at a different time, when they are calm, how they could be supported to use their strategy next time.

136

SESSION 8
Review and reinforce

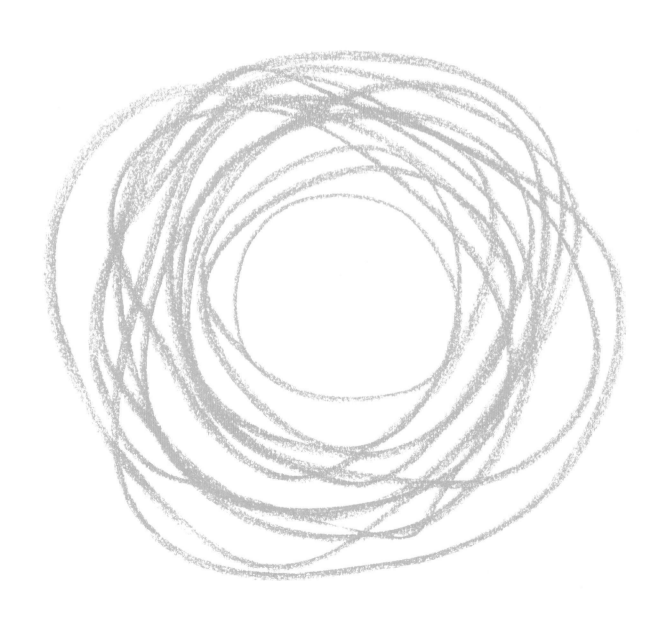

ANGER MANAGEMENT
Session 8
Review and reinforce

Aim

- To think about defensive and threatening behaviours and their consequences (drawing some lessons from the animal kingdom).
- To continue thinking about calming strategies.
- To enable the pupils to know how to apologise when things go wrong.

Resources

- Tokens and rewards (if needed)
- Firework model
- Animal cards or puppets
- 'Animals' worksheet
- Facilitator's animal notes
- 'How to apologise' sheet
- Cooperative picture puzzle

Recap group rules

- Confidentiality; listen and take turns; be kind.
- Reminder of how tokens and rewards can be earned.

Start-up activities

Cooperative picture puzzles – pupils are given one envelope each. Each envelope has a different picture on it. Inside the envelope are some jigsaw pieces which make up the picture. However, only one of the pieces matches the picture on the envelope. The other pieces belong to the other group members. The group must complete their own jigsaw following these rules:

- Work in silence.
- Give pieces away to others.
- Do not ask for, signal about or take pieces away from others.

Review

Review which strategies each pupil chose last week to help manage their anger and whether they were able to use them successfully.

Firework model

Look again at the firework model. Today we will think about the different kinds of reactions we might trigger in others by different behaviours. We can make other people angry or afraid. How we treat others can change how they feel about us.

Animal cards or puppets

Pupils pick a card and complete an 'animals' worksheet for that creature. (There may need to be some discussion first.) What does the creature do when threatened? (How it defends itself.) Does it threaten others and, if so, how? What are the consequences of its behaviour? (See attached chart.) Group members are then given the associated puppet to use as a visual aid when talking about their creature.

Follow-up questions:

- Do you know any people like this creature?
- Which of these creatures are you most like?
- Which would you prefer to be more like?
- What useful defence strategies can we learn from them?

If things go wrong ... how to apologise

Everybody makes mistakes. The important thing is that we acknowledge our mistakes and try to repair the harm we have caused. Apologising is the first step. Discuss the 'How to apologise' sheet. If time allows, pupils could practise apologising through role play.

Plenary

1. Hot seat puppets, or
2. Role play conversations between two puppets about how they behave and interact. Identify positive and negative consequences. What advice would they give to each other and learn from each other?

Rewards

Hand out any tokens and rewards that have been earned.

Animals worksheet

	Name of animal:
	What does your animal do when it is threatened?
	Does your animal threaten others, and if so, how?
	What are the consequences of your animal's behaviour?

Animal sheet – notes for group facilitator

Shark

A shark has a thick skin to protect it from others and attacks first by biting with sharp teeth. However, it is isolated and feared by others.

Hedgehog

A hedgehog is covered in prickles. It rolls into a ball when threatened. It doesn't threaten others, but it doesn't wait to see if others want to be friendly before it rolls into a ball, so it may be quite lonely.

Crab

A crab has a hard armoured shell to protect it and sharp pincers to attack with, so other creatures stay out of its way.

Bee

A bee can fly away or can sting when it is threatened. It can buzz round to scare other creatures. Honey bees will die after they sting.

Tortoise

A tortoise has a hard armoured shell to protect it which it can withdraw into. It does not threaten others and is not feared by others.

Rat

A rat can run away very fast and hide. It does not attack others and only bites if threatened. It is a friendly, sociable, animal and a popular pet.

Dragon

A dragon has a hard skin and attacks others first by breathing fire, biting and using its claws. It is an isolated creature that lives alone in caves as it induces fear in others.

Spider

A spider can run very fast and hide in small places. It traps its prey by spinning a sticky web. It is isolated and avoided by other insects.

How to apologise

Sometimes things will still go wrong, and we may say or do things that will get us into trouble. The quickest way to stop this getting out of control and becoming an explosion is to learn how to apologise.

Timing:

* Approach the person at a suitable time (when they have cooled down and when they have time to listen).

Expression:

* Make sure you have a sorry or sad expression on your face.

Apology:

* Say, 'I'm sorry ...

... that we had a disagreement.'

... that I lashed out.'

... that I upset you.'

(Notice that if the incident was over something that you feel you were in the right about, you are not saying that you are in the wrong, just that you are sorry about what happened.)

Reparation:

* Then ask, 'What can I do to make things right?'

This short apology and reparation can get you out of a lot of trouble – it's that easy!

ANGER MANAGEMENT
Session 8
Review and reinforce

Teacher's feedback sheet

In this session the pupils:

- reviewed how successful they are at using their strategy

- decided whether there are any changes that need to be made to their plan

- thought about the reactions they may get from others by behaving in different ways

- learned how to apologise if things go wrong.

This is important because things will not change overnight: the pupils will need to practise to change their behaviour. They also need to acknowledge that things may go wrong sometimes and to know what to do when this happens.

You can support the pupils' learning by:

- taking opportunities to praise pupils when they manage their anger appropriately

- reflecting with them on beneficial outcomes

- showing confidence in the pupils' progress but accepting that things go wrong sometimes.

ANGER MANAGEMENT
Session 8
Review and reinforce

Parent's/carer's feedback sheet

In this session your child:

- reviewed how successful they are at using their strategy

- decided whether there are any changes that need to be made to their plan

- thought about the reactions they may get from others by behaving in different ways

- learned how to apologise if things go wrong.

This is important because things will not change overnight: your child will need to practise to change their behaviour. They also need to acknowledge that things may go wrong sometimes and to know what to do when this happens.

You can support your child's learning by:

- taking opportunities to praise and reward them when they manage their anger appropriately

- reflecting with them on beneficial outcomes

- showing confidence in your child's progress but accepting that things go wrong sometimes.

ANGER
MANAGEMENT
Appendices

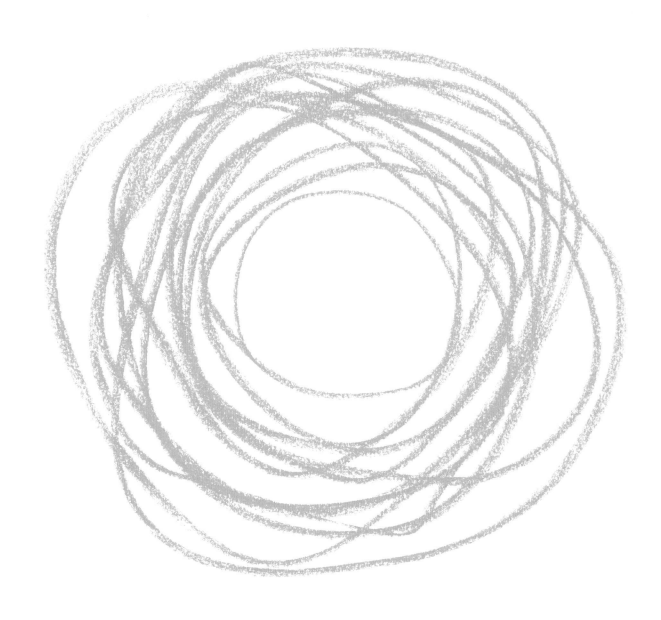

Anger management groupwork flowchart

Referrals for group

Letters to parents

Assess pupil for group. Baselines, motivation, etc

Session 1 Understanding anger → Inform staff how to support work using feedback sheets, etc

Session 2 Understanding feelings

Pupils' supporting tasks

Session 3 Self-esteem → Feelings blog to complete

Session 4 Triggers and fuses → Self-esteem posters to complete and laminate

Session 5 Thinking differently → Anger log to complete

Session 6 Physiology and relaxation → Anger graph to complete

Session 7 Strategies to manage anger → Breathing chart to complete

Try out anger management strategies

Session 8 Review and reinforce

Award certificates and booklets. Pupil evaluations → Work can be shared with rest of class if appropriate

Letters to parents/carers

Outcome measures

Group facilitators meet to evaluate and improve → Make any improvements necessary

Pre-group individual interview sheet

On a scale of 1 to 10, if 1 is not very well and 10 is very well indeed, how good are you at managing your anger and keeping calm?

1   2   3   4   5   6   7   8   9   10

What would you like to be able to do that your anger has stopped you from being able to do?

What things would you like to be different in your life?

In school?

At home?

For yourself?

Would you like to learn how to be able to understand and manage your anger better?

INFORMATION SHEET FOR PUPILS
Anger management sessions

When will the sessions take place?

The sessions will take place once a week in school time for eight weeks.

What will happen in the sessions?

In the sessions we will:

- make things
- talk about anger
- play games
- do role play
- share ideas.

In some sessions we will look at a different part of a firework picture.

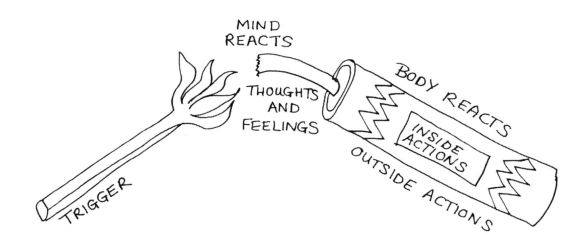

Trigger		The picture has a match, that is, trigger that lights the fuse. In the sessions you will think about 'what lights your fuse' and makes you begin to get angry.
Fuse		The fuse part of the picture is like our thoughts. The way that we think about something can change the way that we feel about it. For example, if you are pushed over you might think that somebody was trying to hurt you. You would probably begin to feel angry. Or you might think that it was an accident. Then you would probably feel less angry. In the sessions we will practise using different ways of thinking about things.
Explosive cylinder		When we feel angry our bodies often give us some early warning signals. We might breathe faster, or feel hot and tense. We will think about some of these signals in the sessions. When we get very angry it can be difficult to think sensibly or think about how other people are feeling. It can be hard to think about the consequences of our actions.
Calming strategies		When we recognise that we feel angry we can use strategies to help us feel calmer. These could include: • walking away • listening to music • playing sports • imagining favourite places. In the sessions we will talk about strategies that could help us feel calmer.

If you have any questions about the sessions you can talk to your class teacher, or myself.

Sample letter to parent

Dear Parent/Carer,

Next term we will be running eight groupwork sessions on social and emotional skills and how to manage feelings such as anger.

We would like to offer your son/daughter the opportunity to take part in these extra sessions, which will take place every week in school for 45 minutes on Tuesday mornings. The sessions will be led by Mrs Smith, our Inclusion Support Manager, and will be supported by the class teacher.

Your child will bring home a feedback sheet every week to enable you to support the work they are doing in the group.

If you have any questions about the group, please feel free to contact either Mrs Smith or myself.

Yours faithfully

Head Teacher

Self-regulation matrix

Learning objective

#	Learning objective	Understand	Recall (remember)	Apply (use)
1	I have learned why people get angry when they feel threatened.	1	2	3
2	I have thought of reasons why it would be good for me to manage my anger better.	1	2	3
3	I have recognised and labelled comfortable and uncomfortable feelings.	1	2	3
4	I have named my strengths and skills.	1	2	3
5	I have learned how to receive and give a compliment.	1	2	3
6	I have identified my triggers for anger.	1	2	3
7	I have learned that there are different ways to think about a situation.	1	2	3
8	I have identified the physical feelings that accompany my anger.	1	2	3
9	I have learned breathing and relaxation techniques.	1	2	3
10	I have learned strategies to manage my anger.	1	2	3
11	I have thought about the impact that my anger has on others and myself.	1	2	3
12	I have learned how to apologise when things go wrong.	1	2	3

Post-intervention evaluation sheet

Please answer these questions about your sessions. Tick the box that shows how you feel.

1. Have you enjoyed the sessions?

Not at all	Not much	Sometimes	Quite a lot	Very much

2. Have the sessions helped things get better for you at school?

Not at all	Not much	Sometimes	Quite a lot	Very much

3. Have the sessions helped things get better for you at home?

Not at all	Not much	Sometimes	Quite a lot	Very much

4. Have the sessions been helpful to you?

Not at all	Not much	Sometimes	Quite a lot	Very much

5. What do you do now that is different?

6. On a scale of 1 to 10, if 1 is not very well and 10 is very well indeed, how good are you at managing your anger and keeping calm?

1   2   3   4   5   6   7   8   9   10

Thank you for completing this form.

This is to certify that

....

Has completed eight groupwork sessions on
Anger Management and has learned:

1. Why we get angry

2. How to recognise feelings

3. What their strengths and skills are

4. What triggers their anger

5. How to think differently

6. How to recognise angry feelings and practise
    relaxation

7. How to manage angry feelings

8. How anger can affect others

Signed ....

Date ....